Reflections on Cambridge

Some Books from Social Science Press

'Good Women do not Inherit Land': Politics of
Land and Gender in India (HB)
NITYA RAO

New Mansions for Music: Performance, Pedagogy
and Criticism (HB)
LAKSHMI SUBRAMANIAN

Writing History in the Soviet Union: Making the
Past Work (HB)
ARUP BANERJI

Political Theologies: Public Religions
in a Post-secular World (HB)
Edited by HENT DE VRIES AND
LAWRENCE E. SULLIVAN
(WITH ORIENT LONGMAN FOR SOUTH ASIA)

Regulation, Institutions and the Law (HB)
Edited by JAIVIR SINGH

Globalization and the Millennium Development
Goals: Negotiating the Challenge (HB)
Edited by MANMOHAN AGARWAL AND
AMIT SHOVON RAY

Cultural History of Medieval India (PB)
Edited by MEENAKSHI KHANNA

Religious Division and Social Conflict:
The Emergence of Hindu Nationalism
in Rural India (HB)
PEGGY FROERER

The Enigma of the Kerala Woman: A Failed
Promise of Literacy (HB)
Edited by SWAPNA MUKHOPADHYAY

Cultural History of Modern India (PB)
Edited by DILIP M. MENON

Delhi: Ancient History (PB)
Edited by UPINDER SINGH

Unbecoming Modern: Colonialism, Modernity and
Colonial Modernities (HB)
Edited by SAURABH DUBE AND
ISHITA BANERJEE-DUBE

After the Iraq War: The Future of the UN and
International Law (HB)
Edited by BERNHARD VOGEL, RUDOLF DOLZER AND
MATTHIAS HERDEGEN

Social and Economic Profile of India (HB)
(In full colour)
PEEYUSH BAJPAI, LAVEESH BHANDARI
AND AALI SINHA

India and China in the Colonial World (HB)
Edited by MADHAVI THAMPI

Everyday Politics of Labour: Working Lives in
India's Informal Economy (HB)
GEERT DE NEVE

Viramma: Life of a Dalit (PB)
VIRAMMA, JOSIANE RACINE AND JEAN-LUC RACINE

Lived Islam in South Asia: Adaptation,
Accommodation and Conflict (HB)
Edited by IMTIAZ AHMAD AND HELMUT REIFELD

Reforming India's Social Sector: Poverty, Nutrition,
Health and Education (HB)
Edited by K. SEETA PRABHU AND R. SUDARSHAN

Human Security in South Asia: Energy,
Gender, Migration, and Globalisation (HB)
Edited by P.R. CHARI AND SONIKA GUPTA

Middle Class Values in India and Western Europe
(HB)
Edited by IMTIAZ AHMAD AND HELMUT REIFELD

Religion and Personal Law in Secular India: A Call
to Judgment (HB)
Edited by GERALD JAMES LARSON

WTO Agreement and Indian Agriculture (HB)
Edited by ANWARUL HODA

Trade, Finance and Investment in
South Asia (HB)
Edited by T.N. SRINIVASAN

Forthcoming

India's Economic Future: Education, Technology,
Energy and Environment
Edited by MANMOHAN AGARWAL

The Story of the Sunderbans: Folk Deities,
Mortals and Exotic Beasts
SUTAPA CHATTERJEE

Hinduism, Buddhism, Islam and Shamanism
Edited by MARIE LECOMTE-TILOUINE

Business and Labour in a Public Sector Company:
Indian Telephone Industries, Bangalore (1948–2006)
Dilip Subramanian

Literature and Nationalist Ideology:
Writing Histories of Modern Indian Languages
Edited by HANS HARDER

'When the War Began One Heard of Many Kings':
South Asian POWs in World War I, Germany
Edited by RAVI AHUJA, HEIKE LIEBAU, AND
FRANZISKA ROY

Reflections on Cambridge

Alan Macfarlane

3/10/09

With best wishes,

[signature]

SOCIAL
SCIENCE
PRESS

Published by
Esha Béteille
Social Science Press
69 Jor Bagh, New Delhi 110 003

Distributed by
Orient Blackswan Private Limited
Bangalore   Bhopal   Bhubaneshwar   Chandigarh
Chennai   Ernakulam   Guwahati   Hyderabad   Jaipur
Kolkata   Lucknow   Mumbai   New Delhi   Patna
www.orientblackswan.com

ISBN 978-81-87358-48-0

Social Science Press thanks Sean T. McHugh (front cover photograph), Borut Peterlin (back cover photographs and those in the text) and Zhiguang Yin (photographs in the text) for their generosity and support in allowing their work to be used in this book.

Set in Goudy
Typeset by Eleven Arts, Delhi 110 035
Printed by De Unique, New Delhi 110 018

For Sarah, companion through my Cambridge years

CONTENTS

LIST OF ILLUSTRATIONS

IN PRELIMS (with captions)

The Woodcut
A teacher addressing an audience of scholars. Books are
scattered around the scene. From these early medieval
origins Cambridge has developed education over a period
of eight hundred years.
The woodcut comes from Christopher Hussey, King's
College Chapel Cambridge (London, 1926) p.22. There is
no indication of what it is, the date, or where it came from.   i

King's Old Bridge and Barge
A view of the Old Bridge of King's College, engraved
by P.S. Lamborn in about 1790.   iii

Ely Cathedral
A few miles northeast of Cambridge city, Ely is even older
than the University of Cambridge. The Bishopric of Ely has
played a protective encouraging role in the development
of the University from its start, and the beauty and music
of Ely complements that of the Colleges.   v

Trinity College Library and the River
West front of the Library of Trinity College designed
by Sir Christopher Wren and built in the later
seventeenth century.   x

Alan Macfarlane Working Alongside Lily in 2004
The two computers and the book-lined study reflect the
change in the world of communications which has been one
of the central features of the author's time in Cambridge.
[Photograph: courtesy Sarah Harrison]   xx

IN TEXT

FRONT COVER PHOTOGRAPH

King's Night
The Chapel is reflected in the Cam, with the Gibb's building
half-obscured by an ancient willow and the bridge under which
punts glide during the day on the right. The buildings are only
occasionally lit up, for example for the BBC recording of the
Christmas Carol Service.
[Photograph: courtesy Sean T. McHugh]

BACK COVER PHOTOGRAPHS

Alan Macfarlane on the Roof of King's College Chapel in 2008 and
King's College Dining Hall
[Photograph: courtesy Borut Peterlin]

PREFACE

When I first set out to write on Cambridge I thought I might produce a brief practical essay to explain how the University works. I realized that over the last twenty years the background of those who came to learn in Cambridge, particularly among the postgraduates, was very different from what it had been in my first twenty years. There are now very many students from outside Britain and even from non-European countries. This latest generation have found that they not only needed to learn new academic skills and theoretical information, but also to navigate through an often unfamiliar (British) culture and a particularly convoluted (Cambridge) set of traditions.

As I wrote for such an audience I began to realize that a possible readership might be not only students from Asia, but also a wider set of friends and colleagues. Many from America or parts of Europe, or even from parts of Britain, seemed to find Cambridge baffling. I remembered that even as a Fellow of King's College from 1971, as a University Lecturer from 1975, a Reader from 1981 and finally as a Professor from 1991, I only gradually began to understand parts of what was happening around me. It seemed worth trying to put my experience into words so that others might be able to take a few short cuts in my company.

I soon discovered that I was also writing a book about something else. This is the question of what helps me, personally, to explore the world, and, more generally, the sources and conditions of creativity and innovation. This is a theme I have pursued over the years and I had long realized that alongside individual factors, the institutional setting makes an enormous difference to what we do with our lives.

As I write this, I am simultaneously doing in-depth video interviews with leading academics, many of them linked to Cambridge, to see how their lives and works fit together and how personal and institutional creativity are linked.[1] This book has become a meditation on the ways in which Cambridge has helped or hindered intellectual creativity over the centuries. Cambridge, a world centre of interesting ideas for half a millennium, is a good place to think about this topic. So this book is also addressed to those who want to know about some of the alternatives open to anyone who wishes to create a social, cultural and political entity which will stimulate innovation, invention and education in the broadest sense.

Another theme which began to emerge is related to a lifelong interest in the question of what the historian E.P. Thompson called 'the peculiarity of the English', which I approached under the title of *The Origins of English Individualism*. Until the last generation, at least, Cambridge University has been quintessentially a very (upper middle class) English place. A study of Cambridge thus allows us to survey distinctive features of the culture, customs, politics and nature of evolutionary change in England. So this book is also for those who are interested in national character and about the deeper tendencies of a civilization which, through its Empire and the United States, has deeply influenced the world we now inhabit.

The theme of 'the peculiarity of the English' was clearly related by my own experience. Oxford and Cambridge cast a downward

---

[1] The interviews described can be seen on *www.alanmacfarlane.com* and some of them are on the 'ayabaya' channel on YouTube.

shadow over the feeder institutions which train people to enter them. I now realize that from the age of eight, at the Dragon School in north Oxford, I was being 'groomed' for Oxford or Cambridge. My mind, in interminable Latin lessons, my body in self-discipline and sport, my hopes and fears, all were being invisibly shaped by a possible goal of Oxbridge entry. I was taught almost exclusively by ex-Oxford and Cambridge teachers and was much influenced by two uncles, both of whom had been at Oxford. The book is also trying to investigate the forces that I have experienced over almost all my life.

Mention of 'Oxford and Cambridge' draws attention to the fact that, while this book is specifically about Cambridge, much of what I say could also apply to Oxford. There are, of course, strong differences, but also family likeness; the two Universities are perhaps closer to sisters than to cousins. Consequently many of my remarks could be phrased as 'Oxford and Cambridge' or 'Oxbridge'. I have avoided this as much as possible as the book is about Cambridge, but this should be borne in mind.

A final goal links to my training as a historian as well as my long-term interest in the 'rescue' aspects of anthropology. Cambridge is changing very rapidly and I know that I live in a very different Cambridge today to that which I joined in 1971. Under the surface of the old buildings and rituals, oral traditions and ways of life are gone in a flash. This is another reason why I am doing the series of interviews of academics, as a kind of oral history, not of a remote non-literate village, but of people at the heart of an advanced industrial society.

So this book also belongs to a genre of accounts of Cambridge at different points of time, among them A.F. Benson's *From a College Window*, E.C. Benson's *As We Were*, Gwen Ravaret's *Period Piece*, Christopher Isherwood's *Lion and Shadows* and Clive James' *May Week Was in June*. It is partly written as a 'period piece' describing a particular experience of the world seen through the eyes of one don in one subject who was a member of one College, mainly recalling what he thought he experienced over the period from 1971–2009.

To future generations it may come to be seen as a sketch of a world which feels unfamiliar yet just recognizable. It may preserve a little of the oral history and traditions of another extraordinarily complex group with whom I have lived.

*

Poets, novelists and anthropologists tend to experience life first and then write about their memories—'emotion recollected in tranquility' as William Wordsworth put it. There is the participation, the fieldwork, the involvement in the flow of time and action. Then there is the retirement, the re-living of events, re-ordering, turning the disorder into a patterned creation.

In these creative acts there has to be a tension, in fact several tensions. As anthropologists put it, we need to be both participants and observers, both inside and outside the action, to feel the pull of the object we are writing about, and yet, to hold it in our conscious and reflective gaze. We need to be close to it, but also to distance ourselves, leaving it, watching it recede, yet not too far off, like sitting in a train or plane after a wonderful holiday recalling all the incidents and sensations.

Cambridge has been one of the most powerful experiences in my life. I have spent thirty-eight of my sixty-seven years in this City and University. I have brought up my children here and began to share it with my grandchildren. I have built up a house and garden where my friends and relatives are remembered in the trees and shrubs. I have taught several generations of students and made many friends. I have lectured, administered and examined, and spent many uplifting moments at films and concerts. I have written articles and books, run research projects, and used it as a base to explore Nepal, Japan, China and elsewhere.

Now I am leaving, or rather vacating my University Professorship and ending my formal teaching in the Department of Social Anthropology. Although I shall remain at King's College and be attached to projects in the University, a long and deeply influencing part of my life, my fieldwork so to speak, is over.

In the brief time when I still partly feel and remember the currents that flow through Cambridge, yet am already relinquishing power and involvement, it feels right to write down rapidly some of my impressions. Two years ago I would still have been too much involved to see the wood I was in, in two years I will have moved on to other landscapes so that the deeper memories and insights will be covered over. It has to be done now or not at all.

This book consequently is a personal set of reflections on what I understand a great university is like during an important part of its history. It is a historian cum anthropologist's semi-professional, yet personal account of what he thinks is the spirit, the hidden dynamics, behind the surface of Cambridge University.

This account is not based on a great deal of extra research, though I have read many of the secondary accounts of Cambridge. Nor have I been through the voluminous primary sources in the Colleges and University archives. I have left these to be mined later. Likewise, the hundreds of files of papers I have accumulated over my years are largely un-indexed and unused here, though they would allow fuller accounts of particular aspects of the story I have to tell. Rather, I have written quickly from the top of my own mind, trying to sketch out the general outlines of Cambridge and how it works.

Clearly this has disadvantages. Despite the input of many friends and colleagues, and the more than seventy long filmed interviews of Cambridge figures which I have made and absorbed, this is largely one person's viewpoint. In fact, everyone's experience of Cambridge, as I shall explain, is very different. If I were younger, or female, or from America, or in another discipline or College, I would have seen it differently. Yet I hope that by setting my experience of Cambridge alongside my anthropological investigations of other cultures in Asia, and of other periods of English history, I have managed to give this account a wider relevance.

I do want to stress that like my explorations of *Japan Through the Looking Glass*, this is a personal exploration, a journey through a partly familiar, partly strange landscape. While I am in Cambridge it mostly seems normal and natural enough. Yet when I look back on it, or sideways at it from some distant continent, it seems extraordinary. It turns into something rather out of this world, anomalous, a time capsule requiring explanation. It is as mysterious as any of the places I visit and work in as an anthropologist. I find myself half aware of what a visitor from China, India, Japan or even America must find so bizarre and puzzling.

As a local inhabitant, a villager in this interconnected world, I want to try to explain it to others, while as an anthropologist I want to capture this unique culture before it mutates into something else, as I see it doing before my eyes.

No doubt, as is often the case in anthropology, the remembering and ordering of intense experiences has a cathartic effect. I have been half in love with Cambridge, admired, adored at times, been proud of, but also, as in all love affairs, have been miserable, depressed, anxious, exhausted and even angry. Cambridge has roused strong and contrary emotions. I want to calm these, to come to terms with the ghosts of my past self and its highly charged experiences. Writing it down is what I have been taught to do when I want to make sense of things, to silence the turbulence.

Whether this book will help others to understand Cambridge either as an abstract phenomenon or as a living space if they visit it or come to study here, I do not know. All I do know is that writing this book has helped to clear my mind and made me understand something of what, at the time, seemed so confused and largely based on unspoken assumptions.

*

Another feature of the book is that it is an attempt to explore the context and background of my own work. It has become fashionable to try to explain the conditions of our intellectual production, to consider more explicitly than hitherto the blinkers which prevent us seeing certain things and which shape our observations of the world. In this effort it is important for me to write about Cambridge.

Cambridge has been my intellectual home for most of my productive years, so its hidden pressures and structures have shaped much of what I have seen and not seen, what I have attempted, my successes and my failures. There have been many other influences as well—my wife, family, friends, travels, books. Yet Cambridge as a place and an institution is undoubtedly a central one. If I had remained at Oxford, or gone to the LSE or to America, I would have done something different. In order to understand myself and my work, I need to explain something about Cambridge.

It was Cambridge that gave me the few years of privileged research time that is a Research Fellowship. It was King's College which over the years made me feel part of an intellectual and social community. It was the Department of Social Anthropology which gave me the excitement of feeling a member of a discipline with a licence to roam where I wished. It was the beauty of this ancient city which gave me moments of elation. It was my room in the Old Cavendish Laboratory which made me feel part of a great tradition of thought.

As I try to explain in the book, the history, politics, customs and culture of Cambridge are unusual and powerful, in sum they both open and close certain doors. While on the journey through the teaching years I was half aware of the pressures and both seized opportunities and accepted the limitations. Now that I am close to a new kind of freedom, but also in danger of a loss of stimulus, I can appreciate more fully both the pushes and the pulls, the positive and negative features of being a player during one-twentieth of the long game of an 800-year-old institution.

I sometimes wonder whether I would have managed better if someone had written a book like this and handed it to me at the start of my time in Cambridge. I am not sure I would. To a certain extent the future experience of young people coming into Cambridge will be different. If my predecessors, for example the Professor of Anthropology, Meyer Fortes, had written a book about how he thought Cambridge worked, I would have found it fascinating, but I am not sure how useful it would have been as a practical guide. The *Inaugural Lecture* on the history of anthropology in Cambridge which Meyer Fortes gave and published is interesting, but there is really nothing in it which I have found helped me much in my daily life in the Department and University. On the other hand, the small book which Meyer was presented with on his election to the Chair by his friend Edward Evans-Pritchard, *Microcosmographia Academia* by F.M. Cornford, has been useful to me and many others over the years even if, as I explain below, Cornford was mistaken in various ways.

It is partly that Cambridge, despite deep continuities, is changing very rapidly all the time. It is partly that only when one has experienced the life, faced the problems, wrestled with the contradictions, that one can understand fully how to put to use the experiences and solutions of others.

Yet we have to believe that we can describe journeys which we have taken and others have not, that we can give pleasure and perhaps understanding even to those who are not involved in our explorations. This book is not a journey up *The Yangtze Gorge and Beyond*, or even *A Short Walk in the Hindu Kush*. Yet it is like those books, an account of travel through space and time in a rather special landscape, told by someone who has made the journey and is now returning from the adventure.

*

My voyage through Cambridge has been enormously enriched by numerous people and only a few of them can be thanked here. I would particularly like to thank all my students over the years at every level, my colleagues in the Department of Social Anthropology and friends and Fellows in King's. I would also like to thank the many people who have been associated with Cambridge and who have allowed me to interview them and learn so much.

During the writing of the book a sumptuous anthology of writings and pictures on Cambridge appeared to celebrate the 800th anniversary of the University in 2009.[2] This book has much valuable information and many accounts of spending time in Cambridge from young and old. Nothing I read in this volume, however, altered my own previous impressions of Cambridge very much, though it did deepen my appreciation of its diversity.

Those who have read parts or all of the book at various stages and given me much good advice include, in no particular order: Maja Petrović-Šteger, John Davey, Peter Burke, Charles Chadwyck-Healey, Sara Shneiderman, Libby Peachey, Peter Jones, Sabine Deringer, Richard Irvine, Sian Lazar, Tina Kosir, Jialing Luo, Xiaoxiao Yan, Kenong Guan, Andrew Morgan, Carla Stang, Tristram Riley-Smith, Zilan Wang, Srijana Das, Jan-Jonathan Bock, Hannah Brook, Paolo Heywood, James Bennett and Michael Lotus. I would also like to thank my publisher Esha Béteille for her encouragement and support in various ways.

In my mind I continue my discussion with the late Gerry Martin with whom I walked and talked over the years. I am also particularly grateful to the Vice-Chancellor of Cambridge, Dr Alison Richard, for not only agreeing to do a film interview on her life, but also for reading the whole book with care at a time when she was particularly busy because of the 800th year anniversary of the University. I also want to thank my family who have encouraged, supported and delighted me over the years in so many ways, in particular my mother Iris and father Donald, Inge and Matt, Astrid, Kate, Lily and Rosa.

As always my greatest thanks go to my wife Sarah Harrison. She helped in numerous direct ways, including reading the book several times with great care and summarizing the interviews. Yet her importance as a co-explorer through my years in Cambridge goes

[2]Peter Pagnamenta (ed.), *The University of Cambridge: An 800th Anniversary Portrait* (Cambridge, 2008).

way beyond this. As always this is much more of a shared book than I can express.

I would like to thank Sean T. McHugh for his generosity in allowing the reproduction of photographs from his website *www. cambridgeincolour.com*, both on the front cover and in the text, as indicated. I also thank Borut Peterlin for the photographs on the back cover and as indicated in the text (*www.borutpeterlin.com*). Zhiguang Yin (*www.semitic.spaces.live.com*) also kindly gave permission to reproduce photographs, as indicated. The references to Willis and Clark are to Robert Willis and John Willis Clark, *The Architectural History of the University of Cambridge*, Cambridge, 1886.

Alan Macfarlane Working Alongside Lily in 2004

HISTORY

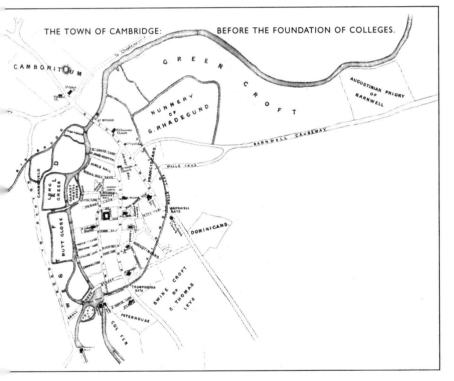

Old Map of Cambridge

A map of the town of Cambridge in about 1200. The shape of the streets
has remained much the same, except for the building of King's and Trinity
which have overlaid Mill Street. The extensive properties owned by various
religious orders were gradually merged into the University and the Colleges
and helped to give an underlying monastic feel to the centre.
[Willis and Clark, IV, fig.1]

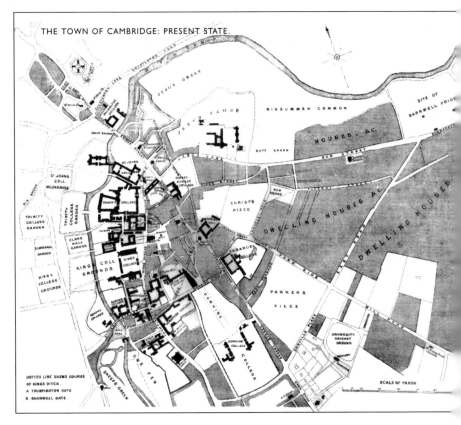

New Map of Cambridge

A map of the town and University in about 1880. The basic shape of the
centre has hardly changed in the last century and a quarter, except that
much of the area adjoining St Andrews Street in the centre and next to
Downing College is now filled with Museums and Science Laboratories.
[Willis and Clark, IV, fig.1]

STRANGE SURVIVAL

I remember that when I went to Oxford as an undergraduate in 1960 I was deeply impressed by the architecture, the traditions and the general feeling of an ancient continuity and stability. It all seemed so self-assured, so self-evidently inevitable, a fact of nature as it was of culture. I felt the same when I became a Fellow of King's College at Cambridge in 1971. In neither place did I have any hint of what I was to discover later, namely that these two universities rather than being the norm are unique in the world. I had no sense that their survival from common European roots was miraculous. Furthermore, it took me many years to realize that much of what I saw around me and experienced in daily life was, in fact, to a large extent a recent invention of the twentieth century laid over a medieval landscape.

The idea of a partly independent institution which is set up to encourage teaching and learning is to be found in most civilizations. There were academies in Greece, Rome, early Islamic civilizations, historic China and elsewhere. Buddhist monasteries or Madrasas have acted in this way, as did the early Christian orders. From this common idea the gradual development of the University in its western form started, some say, in the Salerno school of medicine in the ninth century.

Yet at its inception there was also something new about the university which is unlike any other organization in the world. As Damian Leader points out 'The University was a unique medieval development, separate from the oratorical schools of the ancient world and the scholae of the earlier medieval monasteries.' It is easy not only to merge them with their antecedents, but also to brush away their curious nature by reading back from the majority of modern universities, which are really, again, something very different. As Leader continues, 'medieval Oxford and Cambridge bear, from a constitutional point of view, a closer resemblance to the Worshipful Guild of Fishmongers than they do to the modern University of Sussex.' What this means is that 'these medieval universities must always be seen in the light of the medieval guild or confraternity, and the relation of the scholar to his master as that of an apprentice to an artisan or a squire to a knight. . . . The master was a brother within a mystery; he swore oaths, had privileges, and shared ritual equality with other masters, and they prayed for each other's souls.'[1]

We can see this in the very title by which they are called, namely university. The Latin word *universitas* was at first used for any community or corporation and had to be qualified for several centuries by using *universitas magistrorum et scholarium* to refer specifically to universities. From the fourteenth century the word began to be used alone to refer to what we now mean by universities. These early organizations set the template for all the universities now existing in the world, even though they have departed so much from the originals.

One of the greatest western medieval foundations was the University of Paris, founded in the twelfth century, which to a considerable extent set the pattern which Cambridge followed. Robert de Sorbonne set up a College which is still named after him. However, the Spanish College (a small part of the original

[1]Damien Leader, *The History of the University of Cambridge*, vol. 1 (CUP, 1988), 23.

Sorbonne), founded in 1364 for twenty-four Spanish scholars and two chaplains, is the only College founded in medieval times which, according to Denifle, still exists on the Continent.[2] Oxford and Cambridge, both dating roughly from the period between 1180 and 1210, followed Paris in establishing small residential halls, sometimes under the direction of a senior teacher, where students could live.

European universities tended to be set up in important places, close to the centres of spiritual and secular power. Paris is the quintessential example of this but most continental universities were in big cities where an increasingly powerful Church and State watched their progress with interest. That the two medieval English universities grew up in market towns away from the large cathedrals or biggest cities was strange yet decisive. Innis wrote that 'In England, law and religion were not fortified by universities since these were not located at the capital or in cathedral cities.'[3] The fact that Cambridge was in a rather remote provincial fen town away from London, and some distance from the cathedrals at Ely and Lincoln, helped it to retain its independence. In turn, that isolation meant that power and knowledge were, to a certain extent, separated.

Of the two, Cambridge has always been the smaller town. Despite being a few miles closer to London, it still feels remote in its position on the edge of the fens. We may wonder why it was founded in the middle of an inhospitable part of the country and what attracted the scholars who reputedly left Oxford in 1209 to settle there.

Cambridge is situated where two major roads intersect, one bringing people and traffic from London, the other from Colchester. These roads, Trumpington and Trinity Streets to the west and Regent and Sidney Streets to the east, were built on ancient gravel beds marking an ancient river valley which were the best routes to a river crossing below Castle Hill.[4] The earliest records of Cambridge

[2]*Encyclopedia Britannica*, 11th edition, s.v. 'Universities', 751.
[3]Harold A, Innis, *The Bias of Communication* (Toronto University Press), 21.
[4]I take this point from Peter Searby.

suggest that it was already a quietly prosperous town by the late Anglo-Saxon period and the bridge across the River Cam or Granta, which gave the name to the town, had existed since at least AD 875.[5]

By the time of the Domesday survey in 1086 there was a castle on the hill to the north of the bridge and commercial and residential properties along the river as well as several churches in the main settlement. Through the rivers which drained the whole of the east midlands, traders had access to the inland ports and out to the sea. Cambridge was becoming wealthier and there are today eleven surviving medieval parish churches. There were food markets before 1066, and during the twelfth century there were fairs at Garlic Lane, Midsummer Common and Stourbridge.

Within or near the town were religious institutions, including the canons who moved to a site in Barnwell, and the Convent of St Radegund which had existed since 1135 and later became incorporated into Jesus College. There were two hospitals and seventeen miles to the north was the great Benedictine house of Ely which after 1109 became the seat of a Bishopric.

*

Cambridge University started in a small way. It had no premises of its own and relied on using parish churches, especially Great St Mary's and St Benedict's (or Bene'ts) and on the buildings of the religious orders for public ceremonies. Lectures, disputations and lodgings took place in private houses which provided only temporary accommodation. It appears that quite soon groups of what were known as 'Regent Masters', that is lawyers and theologians, began to build or hire larger places to teach in or house the students. A few of these privately owned and poorly endowed early hostels

---

[5]The following account of early Cambridge is partly based on that on the University website (*http://www.cam.ac.uk/univ/history/index.html*), with kind permission from the University.

survived until the sixteenth century when they were incorporated into the Colleges.

By 1226 the University had a Chancellor and regular courses were taught. In around 1250 a complete set of statutes, which have only recently been discovered, were promulgated, pre-dating the first set for Oxford by about fifty years and well before those for Paris or Bologna.[6] The form of government which they outline is still recognizable today, though it would constantly evolve and change.

From the later fourteenth century onwards, the University began to buy property on the site which is known today as Senate-House Hill, and built the 'Schools' or 'Old Schools' as they are still known. The first building was for the Divinity School, where lectures and disputations took place and there was a chapel, library, treasury and archive. Yet most of Cambridge was still in private hands or belonged to religious houses. From the thirteenth century much was beginning to pass to the new institutions called Colleges, originally for small numbers of advanced students in law or divinity who were to pray for the souls of their benefactors. Later the Colleges began to house the very young undergraduates who had previously lived in hostels or private houses.

*

By the end of the fifteenth century there were seventy-nine universities in Europe, including two in Scotland. Already, however, the shape and ethos of the two English universities was diverging from elsewhere. The obvious mark of this was the wealth and strength of the Colleges.

By 1520 there were in Cambridge thirteen of the thirty-one Colleges that there are today: Peterhouse (1317), Clare (1338), Pembroke (1347), Gonville (1348), Trinity Hall (1350), Corpus Christi (1352), Buckingham College (later Magdalene) (1428), King's (1441),

---

[6]M.B. Hackett, *The Original Statutes of Cambridge University* (Cambridge, 2008).

Queen's (1446), St Catharine's (1473), Jesus (1497), Christ's (1505) and St John's (1511).

Although it was still a rather small and peripheral university, with only seven hundred members in the 1370s, rising to 1300 by the 1450s, the Colleges had come a long way from being merely halls of residence. A glimpse into the regime of King's College in the later fifteenth century shows that they were already a mixture of the social, intellectual and religious, institutions which were almost family-like in their diversity of functions, yet much larger than a family and mostly based on ties other than blood or marriage.

C.R. Fay describes how 'Daily attendance at the chapel services, daily lectures, beginning at six, a strict routine of study tested by a weekly examination, were the lot of every scholar; and even those of higher standing were bound to many duties. The meals were taken together in the hall, the company listening in silence to the reading of scripture; if they did converse it was in Latin. The College not only boarded and lodged its members, it also clothed them, cut their hair and shaved them. Scholars and Fellows were forbidden to sell or pawn their clothes till they had worn them for two years . . . . The College porters trimmed the hair and cut the beards of all the society . . . . No scholar or Fellow, chaplain, or clerk, or other officer might keep dogs, ferrets, or hawks, or throw, play, or shoot within or without the College. Moreover, when the scholars went outside the College gates, they were not to go alone or discard their academical dress; and before they could take a walk into the country, leave of the Provost and Dean was necessary.'[7]

As the Colleges thrived, the University grew more slowly. Indeed, in the extreme case of the very largest foundation of the medieval period, King's College, the scholars could proceed to their degrees without sitting any University examinations, a feature that remained until 1851. In fact, the University was largely a federation of Colleges. We are told that 'Before the middle of the sixteenth

[7]C.R. Fay, *King's College Cambridge* (1907), 54–5.

century, the Colleges began to play a decisive part in University life. They now nominated the Proctors from among their own members for the annual term of office, and their heads often served with the Vice-Chancellor and senior doctors as members of an advisory council which was soon to be called the Caput Senatus. From the sixteenth century until almost the end of the twentieth, the Head of one of the Colleges always held the office of Vice-Chancellor.'[8] In a certain sense, there was no unified and centralized University of Cambridge until at least the end of the nineteenth century.

This was very different from what happened on the Continent and Scotland. There the Universities grew more powerful and the Colleges failed to develop independent wealth through rich endowments or the capacity to teach. The fledgling medieval collegiate systems withered away so that by the end of the eighteenth century only Oxford and Cambridge retained a strong set of independent institutions within a federal structure.

The difficulty of transferring the Cambridge and Oxford system elsewhere is shown by the experiment in America. As Norman Scarfe points out, 'of the 130 University men who migrated across the North Atlantic before 1646, 100 were from Cambridge and no fewer than 35 from Emmanuel, easily the biggest, most influential contingent at work on the mind of New England. They included John Cotton, the leading divine of Massachusetts, and John Harvard . . . .'[9] We would therefore expect that Harvard above all would have a Collegiate structure, later to be imitated by other Ivy League Colleges. Yet although the American universities were called Colleges for some centuries, each being set up by a different denomination, they did not continue or incorporate the Oxford and Cambridge College system. Harvard and others do have associations and clubs, fraternities and sororities, and various social arrangements based on

---

[8]The history of the University on the University website.
[9]Norman Scarfe, *Cambridgeshire* (1983), 93–5.

halls of residence, but the University was strong and no real alternative centres of wealth or teaching were set up.

So there is no equivalent in America today, just as the universities set up in India, Canada and Australia in the nineteenth century, at the height of the British Empire, have not replicated the system. Nor have the waves of new universities in the emerging East Asian civilizations, in Korea, Japan or China, for example, much as they owe inspiration to parts of the European tradition, established anything like the collegiate system.

Even within Britain, the experiment could not be replicated. The early Scottish universities lost their collegiate structure in the sixteenth and seventeenth centuries and now have them only in name or as residential halls. Trinity College, Dublin, which was set up on the Cambridge model and whose leaders were Cambridge men for some time, never really developed a Collegiate model.

In some ways the most interesting case is the University of Durham. Oliver Cromwell wanted to set up a University in Durham, but failed. It was set up as the first new English University by Act of Parliament in 1832 and granted a Royal Charter in 1837. It has Colleges, but they are not self-governing and independent in the same way as those in Oxford and Cambridge, nor do they have the corporate property or much of the teaching role of such Colleges. In general they are responsible for the social welfare of the students. Later universities, the 'red brick' universities of Victorian England such as Manchester, Liverpool and London, and the 'plate glass' universities of the 1960s, such as Kent, Sussex or Lancaster, do not have much beyond halls of residence.

*

It was not just the collegiate system that diverged. There were many notable universities in medieval Europe. A number of them, such as Bologna and Paris, were older and more distinguished than Cambridge. Yet almost all the great medieval universities were seriously weakened or largely destroyed in the period between the fifteenth and eighteenth centuries. In Italy, Portugal, Spain, France and Germany, by the end of the eighteenth century they had lost much of their independence. Royal power, often in league with religious authority, was jealous of the intellectual autonomy and wealth of the old universities. The centralizing absolutisms increasingly undermined them, absorbing their wealth and crushing their independence.

For example, in Germany, at the Reformation in the sixteenth century, the universities became 'instruments of the states . . . their traditional autonomy and freedom disappeared; the professors became state employees; censorship and strict discipline were imposed. The university was regarded as an institution to train functionaries for the state and for the national church attached to it.'[10]

The once independent University of Paris became embroiled in the religious wars of the later sixteenth century and this, along with the growing power of the French monarchy in the seventeenth and eighteenth centuries meant that it gradually fell under the direct control of the Crown. The final blow to an already largely emasculated university occurred in 1793 when the revolutionary authorities abolished all of the French universities. When they were revived in 1808 by Napoleon, they were explicitly State institutions, governed by officials. French academics to this day are civil servants. Little independence either of the University or their constituent Colleges is envisaged in this centralized system. The French universities were not the only ones to disappear. Many of the German universities, including Mainz, Cologne, Bamberg, Salzburg and Erfurt were closed between 1798 and 1815.

This is a widespread tendency and it is not confined to Europe. If we look at the history of independent intellectual institutions throughout the world, whether in the Islamic civilizations of the near East and India, or the Confucian and neo-Confucian worlds of China and Japan, we find that everywhere early shoots of

[10]*Encyclopedia of the Social Sciences*, 1935, s.v. 'Universities', 182.

independence and freedom of enquiry were destroyed. By the eighteenth century there was nothing like a free university anywhere outside north western Europe and North America.

The story of Cambridge is the exception. Somehow it carried the alternative vision of independent centres of power and knowledge through to the present in a continuous eight hundred year arc. This is its greatest achievement, but it was a close thing. Once it was almost totally destroyed, and several times after that nearly trimmed away into mediocrity. Yet in each case a combination of luck, political connections and the broader context of an unusually dispersed system of countervailing powers helped it to avoid destruction.

Subsequently, in the reforms of the universities in the later nineteenth century and nowadays under constant governmental financial and organizational pressures, the universities have had to trim their aspirations. Yet in 1660 after Charles II confirmed the charters granted by his predecessors, Cambridge University was never again under dire threat of being abolished. Throughout the eighteenth and nineteenth centuries many important political figures were educated at Cambridge, including several members of the royal family and leading prime ministers like Walpole and Pitt the Younger. So the threat of total destruction of the autonomous power and privileges of the University was over, although, as we shall see, it is still vulnerable.

*

We can break an answer to the question of what explains the continuous survival and flourishing of this ancient University into several parts. One relates to the internal governance of the University and its ability to change and adapt with the times. I shall consider this ability in the next chapter. Here I want to look at the wider context within which Cambridge operated.

A society or civilization to a certain extent gets the university it deserves. If a society is open, balanced and liberal, it will be reflected in that kind of university. If it is closed, inquisitorial, centralized, it will get another kind. The fact that universities are mirrors of civilizational histories is another reason for writing about Cambridge. In order really to understand Cambridge, we need to know a good deal about the shape of English history from the thirteenth century onwards, and particularly during its formative period up to the seventeenth century.

Cambridge was shaped by a particular intersection of law, politics, economics and religion, parts of which will be touched on in later chapters. Within law, the unique nature of trusts and corporations in English law seems the central determinant. This in turn was connected to a particular distribution of power whereby the Crown could not absorb or undermine the independence of rich and powerful institutions dedicated to education. This in turn was partly based on their economic independence through endowments. All this was later held within the context of an Anglican religious settlement whereby the power of the Church was again limited in a way that was not true of resurgent Catholicism on the Continent, or Calvinism in Scotland.

Within this delicate interplay of forces, the crucial time which could have seen the end of the experiment, but instead saw its flourishing, was between about 1500 and 1800. It was in that period that the wealth and independence of the University of Cambridge and its Colleges was firmly established. Yet it was also the period of the greatest potential threat to its independence.

*

The individual and precarious factors throughout Cambridge history, where the absence of just one person might have led to a different outcome, can be shown in a few of the characteristic moments when the wealth and power of the Colleges was nearly destroyed. If this had happened, Cambridge would now be very different.

The first and greatest threat to Cambridge occurred in the last years of Henry VIII. Elisabeth Leedham-Green tells the story and I shall take my account from her.[11] In the 1530s and 1540s the Crown was busily suppressing the monasteries and appropriating their wealth. The University and Colleges were first visited by Thomas Cromwell's deputy, Thomas Leigh, 'a graduate of King's and notorious as a suppressor of monasteries', in 1535 and were ordered to deliver their 'papistical muniments' with details of all their other wealth. They did this. This was just a prelude, for the Colleges of the University 'were also seen as religious houses, and the vultures looked at them with interest.' The situation reached a crisis in the mid 1540s. 'In 1545 an Act was passed for the dissolution of all major chantries and all Colleges, placing all the foundations in the university at the king's disposal. This was the threat to end all threats. By now the Colleges *were* the university . . . .'

Leedham-Green explains that it is not clear precisely how the Universities avoided ruin. She suggests that the King was persuaded to use local surveyors from Cambridge to save the expense of sending experts down from London. Secondly they appealed successfully to Queen Katherine Parr, whose support was probably gained by Thomas Smith and John Cheke, both royal tutors and taught by John Redman of Cambridge.

College bursars probably made the surveys of College lands and income. The King remarked on seeing their returns that 'he thought he had not in his realm so many persons so honestly maintained in living by so little land and rent'. Questions were raised as to how the Colleges lived in a permanent state of deficit 'to which the reply was made, truthfully if economically, that it was done by the levying of fines on the renewal of leases in those years in which they fell due and by sales of wood.'

The third line of defence 'is obscure in its mechanism but visually pre-eminent in its results'. It seems to have consisted in appealing to Henry's vanity, or fear for his soul, so that instead of

---

[11]See Elisabeth Leedham-Green, *A Concise History of the University of Cambridge* (Cambridge University Press), 47–50.

abolishing the Colleges, he added to their glory. Henry was persuaded to re-establish a languishing foundation of Wolsey's as Henry VIII College (later Christ Church, Oxford). John Redman pointed out that the same effect could be achieved at Cambridge by absorbing three older foundations into one which became Trinity College, and he even found funds for completing Henry VI's lavish chapel at King's.

As Leedham-Green remarks, 'The situation had been saved, and the university as an institution was perhaps never again to face so grave a threat'. The accession of Edward VI in 1548 was hailed by the Protestant party, very strong in Cambridge, and the universities were expressly omitted from the Act for dissolving chantries, that is the chapels endowed for the singing of Masses for the soul of the donors.

That the tradition of intellectual independence should have been saved by the machinations of a handful of well-placed individuals is a good example of how great effects can depend on small causes. It was to happen again in 1997–8 when two or three key individuals, including Roy Jenkins and Tony Blair's old schoolmaster from Fettes, by then Rector of Lincoln College, Oxford, reputedly saved the Colleges from a crippling loss of their tuition fees which might have destroyed the central purpose of a Collegiate university.[12]

The second threat was not on this scale, though it would have seriously weakened the independence of the University if it had not been averted. It occurred when Archbishop Laud was in power in the 1630s. He insisted on his right to visit the universities as Archbishop of Canterbury, to which they objected. 'Cambridge was asked to search its muniments for any privilege exempting them from metropolitical jurisdiction.' Although the University tried to assert its privilege, the King rejected this and it looked as if the visitation would take place. But 'miraculously the threat never

---

[12]For an account of some of the events, see Noel Annan, *The Dons* (2000), 299–301.

materialised, "for", as Laud was to recall, "my Troubles began then to be foreseen by me, and I visited them not"'.[13]

The third occasion was during the Civil War and Interregnum in the middle of the seventeenth century. At the minimum it could have meant the destruction of some of the finest medieval stained glass in the world. In 1644 William Dowsing, Parliament's agent in the eastern counties, was sent to Cambridge to undertake 'the utter demolishing, removing and taking away of all Monument of Superstition or Idolatry'. Pictures and statues were destroyed, chancels were levelled and other trappings smashed. But for reasons unknown, the great windows at King's College were spared. Later the parliamentary general, the Earl of Manchester, descended on the University and various heads of Colleges were removed for refusal to take the Solemn League and Covenant and for other reasons.[14] But basically the University was too well entrenched to suffer more than superficial damage from such activities.

Less well known, however, was a threat emanating from within. Leedham-Green draws attention to the call by the Master of Caius College, William Dell, who had argued against the system of traditional studies, and indeed the very notion of degrees. But she says that he and others 'did not seem to deduce from these premises any necessary diminution in the status of the universities'.[15] She does not refer to something described as follows: 'It was even proposed by William Dell—himself the master of Caius College— to abolish the two universities altogether, as hopelessly pledged to antiquated and obsolete methods, and to establish in their place schools for the higher instruction throughout the country. They were saved, however, by the firmness of Cromwell, at that time chancellor of Oxford . . . .'[16]

*

[13]Leedham-Green, *University of Cambridge*, 70–1.
[14]ibid., 81–3.
[15]ibid., 91.
[16]*Encyclopedia Britannica*. 11th edition, s.v, 'Universities', 771.

Given these accidents and divergences we can see that nothing was inevitable. Saved by a number of curious chances, the University of Cambridge and its Colleges in particular evolved over the centuries.

In the first part of the sixteenth century, King's College Chapel was completed and the grand new College of Trinity was added in 1546, four years after Magdalene absorbed the former Benedictine house of studies known as Buckingham College; Dr Caius enlarged Gonville Hall to make it almost a new foundation, called Gonville and Caius College (1557); Emmanuel (1548) absorbed a Dominican site, Sidney Sussex (1594) that of the Franciscans. These new foundations were concerned with the education of men for the priesthood in the national church, but they, and Trinity especially, attracted for the first time large numbers of lay students.

The University saw another phase of College expansion in the later nineteenth century. The numbers of students doubled between 1850 and 1910 and Colleges started to appoint teaching Fellows, who replaced the private tutors. The supervision system as we know it today was inaugurated. The dons were permitted to marry and retain their Fellowships from 1882. The science faculties began to emerge on what had previously been the botanical garden off Downing Street. There was also the establishment at Cambridge of two Colleges for women students (Girton in 1869 and Newnham in 1872). From the beginning, these Colleges aimed to prepare their students for the Tripos, and the first women were in fact examined in 1882, although attempts to make women full members of the University were repeatedly defeated until 1947.

By 1900, of some twenty thousand university students in Britain about one-third were at Oxford or Cambridge. They were still the dominant universities though now they represent well under five per cent of the student population in British universities. Yet their relative shrinkage was not an absolute decline. The twentieth century has been Cambridge's greatest century in terms of intellectual and artistic contribution to the national life. The story from 1900 to the present is best told in a different way which will explain some of the strange survivals of archaic features that has been the theme of this chapter.

THE CHANGING SAME

One of the most interesting features of Cambridge is the way in which it has both changed and remained the same. In order to survive and thrive over a period of eight hundred years it has had to avoid two tendencies. If it had changed too rapidly, giving way to each new fashion or pressure, it would soon have been unrecognizable. All traces of the past would have gone and it would no longer be its distinctive self.

For example, if all the old buildings had been pulled down as soon as a new style emerged, the current exquisite mixture from across the centuries would not be there to delight us—no King's Chapel, Wren Library at Trinity, Senate House or even Old Cavendish Laboratory. More intangibly, many of its values and practices, for example the College system, the adversarial encounters of the supervision system, the balance of powers in its administration, its diffused ceremonials and minor rituals, would all have disappeared. This could have happened easily at various points in its history. A great deal can occur in eight hundred years. Yet much has been preserved through a certain dogged desire to preserve older things which still seem to work reasonably well—'if it ain't broke, why fix it?'

On the other hand, if there had not been the ability to change, to bend and adapt to time, to emulate a bamboo which retains its shape but can lean with the storms, there would have been an equal danger. Cambridge would soon have lost its connection to the constantly changing national context. The evolutionary growth of England into Britain, from feudal and agricultural to urban, industrial and capitalist would have left it stranded as an anomalous and irrelevant ruin, a time capsule with little function beyond being a museum of quaint people and customs.

So the art is to devise a system which allows change, but only after the implications have been thought through, and where unfruitful modifications die out. An institution such as Cambridge needs to create a way to select sensible and fruitful improvements, while screening out ideas which will damage the roots that feed the system.

Cambridge is like an apple tree which gradually ages, but still continues to bear fruit. If such a tree is sawn down at the base every century, or its main boughs cut away too savagely, it will end up a deformed stump, or something completely different. However if it is not constantly and carefully pruned, the dead wood cut out, to encourage more vigorous growth, it will end up as straggly and produce little fruit. The question then is what are the mechanisms which produce this encouragement and pruning?

*

We can start with Francis Cornford. Cornford was a brilliant classicist who, as a young don in his early thirties, was in favour of some quite fundamental pruning of the University tree and tried, with others, to effect this. He frequently found himself frustrated by conservative opponents. No doubt partly to relieve his frustration, as well as to lay out the rules of the game, he spent a couple of weeks writing a short satire on how University politics worked entitled *Microcosmographia Academica; Being a Guide for the Young Academic Politician*. It was published almost exactly one hundred years ago in 1908.

In less than twenty pages, Cornford warned ambitious young dons that changing the University was a hopeless task and that as they grew older they would in turn become obstacles to change. He described the nature of parties and the differences between a 'Conservative Liberal', a 'Liberal Conservative' and a 'Non-Placet', that is someone who voted against all change. Finally there were the Adullamites, who 'inhabit a series of caves near Downing Street', that is to say the scientists whom Cornford saw as greedy and ambitious.

Cornford described the College system of splitting into small groups to discuss things, the Caucuses. 'A Caucus is like a mouse-trap: when you are outside you want to get in; and when you are inside the mere sight of the other mice makes you want to get out. The trap is baited with muffins and cigars . . . .' Political influence in such a system 'may be acquired in exactly the same way as the gout; indeed, the two ends ought to be pursued concurrently. The method is to sit tight and drink port wine.' The way to lose influence was to publish an accessible book.[1]

What is important for us here is his analysis of why change was impossible. This derives from the simple fact that 'There is only one argument for doing something; the rest are arguments for doing nothing.' The one argument for doing something 'is that it is the right thing to do.' Against this there are two main counter-arguments which always triumph.

One is the 'Principle of the Wedge', which is 'that you should not act justly now for fear of raising expectations that you may act still more justly in the future—expectations which you are afraid you will not have the courage to satisfy.'

The second is the 'Principle of the Dangerous Precedent' which is that 'you should not do an admittedly right action for

[1]Gordon Johnson, *University Politics* (containing complete text of Cornford) (Cambridge, 1994), 97, 99, 102. Cornford's text is available as a free download from the internet.

fear you, or your equally timid successors, should not have the courage to do right in some future case . . . .' This means that 'Every public action which is not customary, either is wrong, or, if it is right, is a dangerous precedent. It follows that nothing should ever be done for the first time.'[2]

These are backed by supplementary arguments. One is 'Give the present system a Fair Trial', though, as Cornford points out, this does not apply to proposed alternatives. The second is that 'the Time is not Ripe' though, as Cornford caustically comments, 'Time, by the way, is like the medlar: it has a trick of going rotten before it is ripe.'[3]

Cornford then shows the tactics employed in 'The Conduct of Business' to prevent any change occurring. These include the arguments that 'The present measure would block the way for a far more sweeping reform.' Another is that 'the machinery for effecting the proposed objects already exists'. Furthermore, 'it is far better that all reform should come from within' which is also known as the 'Principle of Washing Linen' (which should be done in private).

He lists the techniques for destroying arguments for change—the methods of prevarication, of setting up weak arguments and then destroying them, the suggestion that the proposal was put forward some years ago and was rejected then, or of boring the listeners into submission. This last method is the art of talking 'slowly and indistinctly, at a little distance from the point' so that everyone will vote with you rather than listen to you a moment longer.

Some sixty years after Cornford, but very much in his spirit, Jasper Rose and John Ziman suggested that 'Oxbridge does not breed missionary zeal. The preservationist atmosphere, the traditions, the ceremonies, the legacy of the past to be loyally guarded and bequeathed unharmed to posterity—all these crush any capacity for imaginative social action. There are rebels, but they are eventually

[2]ibid., 105.
[3]ibid., 105.

checked and frustrated. There are liberals, but their liberalism is often so old-fashioned, so mechanical, so unradical, that they are only a convenient foil for the explicitly conservative.'[4]

Rose and Ziman describe a conservative situation, with very little power at the centre and not much instituted authority or sanctions. Each don faces in a different direction and is indeed divided within him or herself. Many are the times I have found my mind pulled back and forth in a meeting, half in favour, half against every proposal. I can see what they meant when they wrote 'those who live and work in Oxbridge are pulled in different directions, distracted by conflicting loyalties, distressed by the incoherence in their institutions. Any attempt at change, whether forward, backward or sideways, is baffled and frustrated by the rigidity induced by these conflicts. The logs are all pointing different ways, and jammed tight together in an amorphous mass.'[5]

Cambridge is old and complex because of the accretions of rules and customs and the distributed nature of power. There are bound to be strong vested interests in retaining tried and working practices. Cambridge is set up as a devolved system of power so that there are many people who have a say in decisions, and it requires wide consensus before anything can be changed. Most people have to agree to the change. Often they have to forgo their narrow partisan advantages for the greater good, giving up some present benefit for the sake of a wider and more uncertain future one.

*

Yet one of the most striking features of Cambridge is the way in which the whole system has managed to absorb new changes in a short period—while keeping its core relatively unchanged. The Cambridge I came to in 1971 seems very distant from the Cambridge I know in 2009. Related to this is the way in which Cambridge

---

[4]Jasper Rose and John Ziman, *Camford Observed* (1964), 127.
[5]ibid., 211.

covers over its tracks. What has astonished me is how new is much of what I encountered—and yet I assumed at the time to be old. My students and even my younger colleagues are amazed to find that much of what 'Cambridge' is like now has been invented in the last century or less.

For the strange fact is that Cornford was mostly wrong. There has been immense change since he published his devastating account. As Gordon Johnson writes 'In many respects, it requires a real effort of the historical imagination to conjure up the Cambridge of the young Francis Cornford'.[6] It is worth briefly listing some of the changes which have totally transformed Cambridge in the last hundred years.

He would recognize the central College area, but be amazed at the expansion of the city, with its new shopping precincts, airport and bi-pass. Also the University has been transformed physically. It now effectively has three campuses with two large developments on the Sidgwick site and the west Cambridge science faculties, as well as a new concert hall, library on the other side of the river, and a huge new hospital, and a ring of science parks around the city.

Cornford fought to reform the government of the University. Since his time a great deal has changed. The Regent House has replaced the Senate House as the final governing body, returning power to the actual teachers within the University rather than all those who have passed through it. The Vice Chancellor has become the executive as well as ceremonial head of the university and there are numerous pro-vice-Chancellors. Faculties and Faculty boards which did not exist in Cornford's day are a basic unit of administration and now Schools and Councils of Schools are rapidly gaining power. Most of the Departments and Centres have been created since his time, many of them since the Second World War. A number of new Colleges have been founded, including a new women's College and several entirely secular foundations. The

[6]Johnson, *University Politics*, 83.

financial organization is immensely more complex and after 1919 the University became dependent on government subsidies for the first time.

The organization of teaching and research has altered hugely. Cornford was writing just as honours degrees were starting to outnumber 'pass' degrees, and now the former are almost universal. When Cornford wrote his book there were thirteen Triposes or courses of study; there are now over fifty. More than five times as many undergraduates matriculate each year. There were no postgraduates in Cornford's day. The Ph.D. was only introduced in 1919 and did not become at all common until after the Second World War. Now there are several thousand students doing Ph.D. degrees. There were no taught master's courses in Cornford's day but now there are more than eighty.

The nature of the undergraduate body has also been totally transformed. In Cornford's day it was all men (though two women's Colleges did have students who were allowed to study to a certain extent alongside the men, but not properly recognized). Now half of the students at all levels are women and, starting in 1972 with several Colleges, all the men's Colleges have become mixed. This has had enormous effects on every aspect of life in Cambridge, including, among other things, widening the range of artistic life in drama, music and sports.

Almost all the students in Cornford's day were from Britain, now a very large proportion, especially at the postgraduate level, are from abroad and increasingly from far away, particularly from Asia. Those from Britain are different too. In his day they were almost all from the middle class and from private boarding schools. Now over half the intake, and in the case of some Colleges three-quarters, are from state schools and from all social classes.

Finally, the intellectual and artistic flowering of Cambridge in the twentieth century would have amazed him. For example, in drama the Footlights were already present and performance of plays went back to the sixteenth century, but the enormous flourishing, particularly in the period of the 1960s when much of the talent in British television and satire came from Cambridge, would not have been predictable. Or again in music, the great period of choral singing had not occurred. The same is true in almost all fields—literary criticism, political science, chemistry, astronomy, computing and many others. The Nobel Prize had only just been awarded for the first time seven years before the publication of Cornford's book. He would have been amazed and rather rueful to find that the 'Adullamites' whom he scorned were to win over eighty such prizes in the next hundred years.

So how, against Cornford's prophecies, did all this happen, alongside so many other things such as the almost complete disappearance of gowns after dark and the university police or bulldogs? Even punting along the Backs, such a quintessentially 'Cambridge' tradition, was not present at the start of the twentieth century. What we need is the other side to Cornford's picture, in other words the mechanisms and institutions which allow Cambridge to change very fast indeed—and yet, as Johnson says, to preserve something, for 'despite the colossal changes wrought by the twentieth century it is remarkable how much of the old Cambridge survives.'[7]

*

We find the answer in a number of areas. One is the force of reasoned argument. Cambridge is dedicated to teaching that good arguments trump bad ones. The very Adullamites, whom Cornford feared, encourage this feature. Many of them have risen high in the University and have applied their ideas of sifting bad arguments from good and love of experiments to the Colleges and Committees which they have run.

The system of oppositional arguments, as in supervisions, leads to several effects. There is ingenuity in outflanking problems so that as the contradictions and blockages which continuously face an

[7]Johnson, *University Politics*, 83.

organization through time occur, there are many trained minds applied to solving these in creative and ingenious ways. There is a respect for well-argued cases. Furthermore, a teaching and research environment which promotes an atmosphere of adversarial challenge and constant questioning means that everything is a temporary and provisional solution. There are no sacred truths, everything is debatable, and there are no final answers.

Cambridge is, in Karl Popper's words, an 'Open Society', constantly testing, improving, and striving towards a never-finalized 'truth' or 'beauty'. There are always better solutions waiting in the future. Cambridge, while respecting and wanting to preserve what is good from the past, also looks forward. The future holds, through rational argument, a better outcome.

*

This links to a certain egalitarian ethos within the circle of those who are its members. Part of Cornford's pessimism arose from the fact that he thought that all radical ideas would come from those of his own age or younger. These people would not have 'weight'. Yet I have seen that junior Fellows are listened to attentively and their ideas often accepted, and that even student representatives can persuade Fellows (whose mean age may be fifty or more) to do something. Within the forum, all are largely judged on their arguments rather than their longevity. Just as I listen and am forced into agreeing with my students as they present compelling arguments in supervisions, so my intellectual training makes me respond to what is said and not who says it.

Another important technique is used to overcome Cornford's acute observation that, on the whole, nothing should be done for the first time. Clearly if this were the trump card there would be no science parks, no women's Colleges, no postgraduate degrees to name but three. What we find, however, is that there are almost always real or invented precedents for new departures. It can be made to look as if one is going back to something earlier, while in fact it is new, what anthropologists have called 'the invention of tradition'.[8]

One example is the Advent Carol Service at King's College. This was devised in 1934 by Eric Milner-White then Dean of King's. It feels very old because he took a number of early carols and readings from the Bible. The service has continued every year and become a national institution. To prevent the service from decaying, each year it is subtly altered with new carols and settings. The form remains constant but the content changes.

*

It is not difficult to devise a set of matching arguments alongside Cornford's. For example, 'the time is not ripe' is matched by 'the window of opportunity' argument. I argued recently against spending large sums of money on a building because (given a looming economic recession), the 'time was not ripe', though in a somewhat different way to Cornford. This was matched (and defeated) by the proponents of the scheme who argued that precisely because of the economic situation, this was a 'window of opportunity' because builders would be eager for the custom and perhaps lower their prices.

The 'thin end of the wedge' argument can be countered by the 'stitch in time saves nine'. One can argue that a small reform now will patch the system and mend things so that much larger changes are avoided in the future. This I have often observed in dealing with student demands. If they ask for reasonable small changes it is sensible to accept these rather than build up resentment and a growing desire on their part to make much more fundamental demands.

Part of this relates to the generally consensual nature of Cambridge micro-politics. The price of efficiency and unity is

[8]Eric Hobsbawm and Terence Ranger, *The Invention of Tradition* (1983). It may be no coincidence that Hobsbawm was from Cambridge and Ranger from Oxford.

that people are often quite pliable, deferential to the Chair of the meeting, unwilling to stick their necks out and be thought of as awkward customers.

If people are known to be wary of innovations, one can use a variant of what the Japanese call 'root binding', that is preparing people for changes by patiently explaining to them the implications and advantages of the reforms, getting them on your side, soothing their anxieties, and doing this over a period so that when the change occurs it is already absorbed and people are happy about it.

Another element is the balance of a system which has numerous entities, all more or less on the same level of power. If one Faculty Board or College blocks something others may try it. So diversity is encouraged, and creativity in the face of ongoing problems is possible. This is both conscious and random, and then, as Charles Darwin showed, there is a mechanism of natural selection which keeps better solutions. The late comers soon find themselves forced into a change which they blocked earlier on.

An example from my own experience is partly about this. When the University announced it was prepared to introduce new taught Master's courses, quite a few Departments and Faculties showed little interest. Teaching on such courses was not to be remunerated. It was just more work for already busy people. But our go-ahead Professor saw an opportunity which might lead indirectly into more power and income and the propagation of our discipline. So we were among the first to set up a Certificate and then an M.Phil. with various options. Within fifteen years we were told to cap our numbers because everyone wanted to offer such courses.

Another feature is that with a consensual system of politics, much of the business in crowded meetings goes through without any kind of argument or vote. It is very easy to smuggle through small changes all the time without anyone really noticing, or if they do, they feel that someone somewhere must have scrutinized this carefully. Indeed the matter has often come out of the report of a subcommittee set up a year earlier and consisting of two or three people whose recommendation, perhaps with two in favour and one against, can be passed by a much larger body without much discussion.

In such a world, a powerful personality with plenty of energy, skilled in local politics, with good connections and a great deal of knowledge of the system and of previous history can effect a stream of minor changes. I watched such a person over a period of five years fundamentally change our small Department (having set it up a year or two earlier) without too much hindrance or impediment. There are several accounts of such changes in the interviews I have done, for example in biology and zoology in the second half of the twentieth century. A handful of individuals can set up whole new centres, faculties and other organizations and change the content of teaching and research. Their success shows the inner dynamism of what looks at first an unyielding and preservationist institution.

*

Cambridge is a secure environment within which to take risks. Given the accumulated prestige and solidity of the organization, it is possible to try out new things. I noted this early in relation to King's College which was innovative in terms of taking women, in widening its student intake and in altering its social and ritual arrangements. It could do this partly because the College reputation was so great that a mistake or two would not bring it down.

Douglas Adams (was he thinking of Cambridge where he had been a student?) wrote in *Hitchhiker's Guide to the Universe* that the earth is a giant experiment or computer set up by some white mice. In Cambridge the experiment has been running for eight hundred years. Through selective mechanisms the University has visibly improved, though at certain points it blundered off down various non-productive tracks. It has the ability of self-renewal. This is unusual since thoughts and institutions have a strong tendency to wither through time as their purpose is lost and their members become out of touch with the outside world.

I believe that if Cornford had been living at this hour (he died in 1943) he would have been amazed and probably delighted that he had been so wrong. Despite the many arguments for not doing things, the one argument for doing them—that they are the right thing to do—has prevailed widely, and yet in a measured way. This balance has preserved this unusual place well enough to enable it to delight and enchant many of those who visit, teach or are educated here.

*

If I were asked what the secret of striking a good balance between innovation and continuity is, I would point to a localized example of a very widespread English feature. This is the importance of unwritten, oral, customary norms based on common sense and a respect for precedent. This is an old feature of English law, as shown in the thirteenth century work of Henry de Bracton *On the Laws and Customs of England*. The way in which customs give flexibility yet stability is excellently shown in the local context of Cambridge.

It is relatively easy for customs to change, since they are not written down and anyone can say 'we've always done it like this', and if it suits the listeners, then small changes occur. This is one of the ways in which Cambridge constantly shifts, alters direction, grows and evolves, yet appears not to be doing anything other than what it has always done. New people feel that the ways of doing things they encounter must have been there for ever, until they suddenly disappear.

On the other hand, customs prevent large changes, revolutions, massive and swift alterations. The main justification for things being as they are is that they have always been like this. Big organizational changes are against the customs and have difficulty in being implemented since they are clearly new and not customary. It is like a giant game—to suddenly change the rules, it is widely believed, will lead to unfairness, instability and quite likely to ruin. If life is like cricket or rugger, you can't just come in and change the rules.

In countries and organizations with a written set of rules, one authority can alter the written constitution and everything is changed. With customs, it is necessary to alter thousands of small, implicit, practices in order to achieve any significant change. So there is a bias towards slowly evolving and continuous growth. It is certainly not centrally planned. Cambridge moves by evolutionary modifications rather than by the punctuated equilibrium of more rigid, explicit, institutions. It is random variation and selective retention.

It is true, as Cornford argued, that customary systems give a bias towards the longer dwelling and older inhabitants. The 'young man (or woman) in a hurry' who wants to change things is new to the jungle of intertwined customs; he or she cannot absorb many of them until after a few years. It is difficult to change much at a deeper level, although he may gain small victories. After twenty years, when one understands the customs and speaks the local 'language', the strong investment one has in the system, the sense that one has heard all the arguments for change and tried things which work no better, often becomes overwhelming. Institutional conservatism is built into the system.

Yet custom is also liberating, for inconsistency is masked and plural worlds are possible. Customs can clash, contradict, be out of step, yet work. It can be a custom that only Fellows walk on the grass—until a children's day is held or a May Ball when everyone tramples on it. It may be a custom that only people with a High Pass are accepted onto a course until someone argues heatedly that a brilliant student who failed altogether should be allowed to continue due to special circumstances.[9]

Customs are largely an extrapolation backwards of what is currently being done, but the reasons have never been clearly

---

[9]Peter Burke tells me that at New College, Oxford, where there were rules about pets, a prohibited dog is said to have been defined as an allowable cat because people liked the owner.

enunciated or are lost in history. They fit in a world of a kind of ancestor worship. If wise heads in past centuries thought a way of doing things worked, that standing on the slippery end of a punt was better than doing what they do in Oxford (which is to stand more safely in the sloping and protected area), who are we to argue?

A customary approach also fits well with a complex system. It would be impossible to map how the Cambridge system works in a set of diagrams or rational equations. As Alexis de Tocqueville wrote of English law, so it can be said of Cambridge, which 'may be compared to the trunk of an old tree on which lawyers have continually grafted the strangest shoots, hoping that though the fruit will be different, the leaves at least will match those of the venerable tree that supports them.'[10] The result is that, according to Tocqueville, in France there is simplicity, coherence and logical organisation, whereas in England there is an 'old-fashioned and monstrous machine' with its 'complicated and incoherent plan'. Yet, as Tocqueville acknowledged, in England there has been liberty, while in France the ever-present threat of authoritarian absolutism.

Also, the very complexity of this ancient and convoluted system, which makes it so difficult to bring about revolutionary and sweeping change, makes evolution easier since no single clique or group can control the whole of the system, as we will see in the competition between Colleges or Faculties for primacy. Through the sort of mechanisms which Darwin described, through random variations and selective retentions, evolutionary change and the survival of the fittest ideas can be ensured.

---

[10]Alan Macfarlane, *The Riddle of the Modern World* (2000), 205.

CULTURE

Cambridge University and City Centre from above

St Mary's Church is on the left, King's Chapel on the right and the Senate House and chestnut tree in the centre. Many of the important developments in human thought in the last half-millennium occurred within a quarter mile of this area.

CHARM AND GHOSTS

When you visit Cambridge on a beautiful summer's day, or when the snow covers the antique roofs, you are almost bound to be charmed and perhaps entranced. I feel the same after many years in Cambridge. The place feels as if it is indeed bewitched and magical. Where does this special effect lie?

We are attracted to places which allow our minds and imaginations to expand. Many visitors know that Cambridge is old— but how old is it? Parts feel very ancient, but beside them are obviously newer and even very modern features. Cambridge seems ageless and yet is also constantly modified and restlessly changing. It is impossible to confine it into any particular period.

What we experience leads the mind out of the present, across the bridge of the twentieth and nineteenth centuries with its industrial revolutions, back through to the classical forms of the Enlightenment. It does not end there, however, for we move through Tudor courts and towers in the winding alleys back into the soaring arches and narrow windows of the medieval world. To walk into Cambridge is to enter a time machine.

The close juxtaposition of very widely separated architecture can be comfortably absorbed because there are gaps, lawns and trees and courts which separate the buildings. So you can stroll through a checkerboard of English history, see all its styles and periods laid out in an irregular yet controlled and calm fashion.

As you walk you will sense that the ideas of each of the periods over the last eight centuries are not only to be found embalmed in stone and wood and glass. They survive inside these buildings in styles of philosophy, poetry, music, mathematics or theology which are still alive. While Francis Bacon and Newton and Darwin and Maxwell are gone, their descendants are still around, perhaps as direct lineal descendants—a Huxley grandson, a Darwin great-grandson, a John Maynard Keynes nephew or niece, but more often in people who wrestle with similar problems.

Cambridge also has the charm of a place which is not quite real. It is light, open, inviting, and yet constantly elusive, like Keats' maiden after whom the suitor follows 'in mad pursuit' but never attains. The day visitor or even the undergraduate feels that there are depths and riches, stores of buried knowledge and experience, a thick web of stories and legends here. Yet these are only glimpsed, shadows, disappearing round a corner or along a sunbeam.

There is nothing threatening about the place, though it can fill a person with a certain awe. The architecture is mainly accessible and much of it is informal. It is like a Christmas card or a grouping of small country houses. It is on a human scale, with most buildings only a couple of floors high.

*

You may think that it is just a coincidence that the two great medieval English universities are threaded by rivers and incorporate a ford and a bridge in their names. Yet it seems increasingly obvious to me that this connection with water is part of the secret of their special nature.

Willows by water, boats on water, clouds in the water, buildings reflected over the water, bridges curving over water are among the most enduring images of Cambridge. The most famous expression of this, I have only recently discovered, is in the poem which every school child in China learns.

A two-ton slab of Beijing white marble (the stone used to build the Forbidden City in Beijing) was inscribed with four lines of poetry in Chinese and placed at the end of the Bridge at King's College in July 2008. This commemorates Xu Zhimo who, as an associate of King's College for two years from 1920, wrote his 'On Saying Good-Bye to Cambridge Again'. The second version of 1928 begins with the following verses.

Very quietly I take my leave
As quietly as I came here;
Quietly I wave good-bye
To the rosy clouds in the western sky.

The golden willow by the riverside
Is the young bride in the setting sun;
Her reflection on the shimmering waves
Always lingers in the depth of my heart.

My Chinese students tell me that the watery landscape of Cambridge and the Fens is what attracts them most, perhaps evoking the famous Chinese landscapes of the mountains and rivers and water margins of China, the mighty Yangtze, the mists of Guillin or the canal cities of the eastern seaboard. This is one of the reasons why this poem, and Cambridge with it, has become so famous in China.

The river Cam does many things for Cambridge, although it has ceased to be the great thoroughfare for traffic via the Ouse from all over England, bringing goods up through Cambridge and to Stourbridge Fair on the outskirts of the city.

The river is a thread, joining together the Colleges along its banks, buildings on one side, gardens and lawns on the other— Peterhouse, Queen's, King's, Clare, Trinity Hall, Trinity, St John's,

Magdalene—the pearls on the green string gain much of their grace from the river quietly flowing past.

Likewise the bridges, from the mathematical bridge at Queen's with its mythical links to Newton, King's, Clare, Garret Hostel, Trinity, St John's, the Bridge of Sighs modelled on that in Venice, Magdalene, both separate and join the city. Beauty lies in balance and contrast. To have a green central space where white cows and geese graze the rough turf and swans swim on one side, and the smoothest of lawns and mighty buildings on the other, creates a special delight.

The Cam also links Cambridge to its region. It is the upper reach of a set of waterways which go down through the Ouse and flow out to the sea. It constantly reminds me that Cambridge town is older than its University, and that this small University is just a part of the mighty system which connects with Ely and with Holland and the drainage of the Fens, and out through the Wash. Water helps to diminish the provincialism of this remote place and link it to the whole world.

'Only connect', as another Cambridge figure, E.M. Forster, used to put it, and Cambridge is full of connections once the mind is set free. Water is the great connector. It connects the huge wet skies of Cambridge to the black peat soil and the reedy fens. Water links the springs of the Cambridge uplands in the mysteriously named Gog and Magog hills to the mill at Trumpington about which Chaucer wrote, and then the mill at Grantchester where Rupert Brooke set his poem and the church clock no longer stands at ten to three.

The river connects Grantchester Mill through the long meadows to Cambridge past Laundress Lane, where precious manuscripts of a long-lost British Empire are combed by scholars, past Samuel Pepys' marvellous library. The river goes on through the meadows where medieval fairs and gatherings of gipsies are still remembered in 'Strawberry Fair' on Midsummer Common, in circuses and bonfires on November 5th, and then out into the fens down to the magnificent cathedral of Ely, known as the Ship of the Fens.

In Oxford, I remember that the Cherwell and the Thames did something similar. Woven with my memories of the Cam are others of early May mornings by Magdalene Tower, of lingering along the river in the Parks, of learning to swim in the chilly waters of the Cherwell, of skating on Port Meadow as a child, of punting out along that river, and of catching my first fish in the Oxford canal. The rivers in Oxford are grander, though they do not run quite so directly through most of the big Colleges.

The presence of water gives life to the buildings because it is constantly moving, both with its internal force and as a mirror of the skies and winds. I find that the beauty of the changing years and the excitements of my changing intellectual discoveries are caught in this ever-flowing river. It also adds to the sense that Cambridge is like an ancient stately home, Blenheim or Stowe, where lakes and rivers are used by the architects to give a sense of that ordered wildness which the English love.

*

As I remember Cambridge from afar, the colours are muted. They are the mellow brown of sun-warmed walls, the greys, whites, and pale pinks of all varieties of stone from Wales, from Yorkshire, from France. There are the blacks of gowns. It is mostly a sepia landscape, like an old photograph.

Yet, against this restrained background there are sudden vivid splashes. There are the red and yellow tiles shipped from Holland. There is the vivid green of budding willows, the scarlet of academic gowns at feasts and the impossible blue of summer days over the soaring pinnacles of King's.

So Cambridge is a sober place, full of subtlety and rich with shadows, infinite varieties of grey or green or blue mixed together. Yet there are bright roses against grey walls, a brilliant flag flapping on a College roof to celebrate or to mourn, the yellows of the aconites along King's walk and the pools of purple crocuses behind Trinity. All come together in the incomparable miracle of the blended bubbles of light in the stained glass whose imperfections soak up and soften the glow of the sunlight in the splendour of King's.

As with much of Cambridge, there is both unity and variety, which gives the eye rest and pleasure in constant renewal under the ever-changing skies and through the very marked seasons. And most wonderfully for me are the accidental colours, as when I walk along the back of King's and see all the ancient windows turned into sheets of burnished gold by the setting sun.

John Betjeman beautifully catches the effect.

The white of windy Cambridge courts, the cobbles brown and dry,
And umber plaster Gothick with ivy overgrown—
The apple red, the silver fronts, the wide green flats, and high
The yellowing elm trees circled out on islands of their own—
Oh, here behold all colours change, which catch the flying sky
To waves of pearly light that heave along the shafted stone.

Across this stage, the colours of the entire world flow, saris and tartans, grave suits and skimpy shorts, faces from every continent and voices speaking many of the languages of the world. They drift like blown confetti through the old buildings and streets and then are gone and the University settles back into its monastic routines, apparently unchanged.

Yet Cambridge is constantly changing. The bookshops come and go, the cranes rise and build new shops and arcades, but the core remains, a new building here or there, a refurbishment, a set of new cycle ways, but the deep grammar of colour and form is not totally altered.

The tensions between an artificially preserved 'heritage' site, neat but dead on the one hand, or being swamped by change, is reasonably managed and is, I suspect, one of the attractions of Cambridge. Visitors are aware that this is not just a Museum, a Mausoleum, a Stone Henge or Great Wall of China. The druids are still very much in business.

*

In his 'Stones of Venice', John Ruskin draws attention to the irregularity and spontaneity of English art. He contrasts continental, Baroque, art with its formal gardens, central plaza, heavy classical-style buildings and straight streets—authoritarian, planned, dominating—with the crooked, asymmetrical, unbalanced, lightly planned art of the Gothic north.

Cambridge is a fine example of what Ruskin is talking about. It is illustrated in the poetry, for instance in the line by Rupert Brooke when he compares the German flower beds where everything is in neat lines to the 'sweet disordered English rose' which grows as it will. It is shown in the jumbled nature of many Cambridge Colleges, styles from different centuries thrown together.

The whole place is a hotchpotch of styles and conceits. Yet this is what gives the lightness, surprise and dynamism, the unresolved tensions of Gothic art. Here it seems to me that Cambridge contrasts quite considerably with Oxford. My own College, at Oxford, Worcester, feels quite like Cambridge but many of the larger Colleges there, such as Christ Church and Magdalene, are much heavier and more portentous.

This sense of contrast is what Nikolaus Pevsner considered to be at the heart of Cambridge architectural aesthetics. 'Now the aesthetic character of Cambridge is one of variety and intricacy. Large and small, monumental and intimate, stone and brick, man-made and nature-made stand close to each other and often interwoven with each other. Small court follows large court, turfed court follows cobbled court, open court follows closed-in court.'[1]

*

The Gothic tensions of sweeping asymmetry reach their highest expression in King's College Chapel. It somehow feels unfinished, still soaring and aspiring, impossible in its distribution of forces and its absence of flying buttresses, in the huge weight apparently carried along its slender fan vaulting and columns. It feels like a paper

[1]Nikolaus Pevsner, *Cambridgeshire* (2nd edition, 1970), 38.

lantern floating in the fens, especially when the light streams through the highly irregular and crooked gleaming jewels of its stained glass. It is dream-like yet solid, lifting the whole city into the wide grey skies. It draws the eyes across the meadows and is balanced in a strange way by the straight lines of Clare College and the Gibbs Building.

The northern, crooked, energetic Gothic world that grew after the collapse of the Roman Empire is preserved in Cambridge as a constant reminder of something which stands apart from the constant tendency towards bureaucratic rationalization, centralization and the demand for homogeneity and standardization.

The crookedness applies not just to the buildings, but to everything I have experienced in Cambridge. The regulations of the University, the arrangement of the teaching system, the lay-out of the streets, the shape of the river, the cacophony of different arts, all are distinguished by variety, asymmetry, a jumble of bits tacked onto other dissimilar bits. The only synthesis is provided by the resolution of opposing forces.

Cobbles are used on roads, paths and courtyards. They are small round stones, each distinct and separate, set in the ground, sometimes now with cement but originally, as those outside the front of King's College, packed tightly together. It is a form of robust covering which pre-dates tarmac and the smooth surfaces of modern roads. Pebbles and flints in the walls down the smaller streets of Cambridge are also old.

The artificial preservation of both of these forms of building materials in many parts of Cambridge, for example in one of the oldest parts of a preserved building, the thirteenth century back of Corpus Christi College in Free School Lane, are often a self-conscious anachronism. They give a sense of medieval antiquity, of a quiet, bumpy, world where the streets were also cobbled and the wheels of carriages or bicycles were the only ones to be found.

Where there are not cobbles there are paving stones—as in the streets, courtyards and elsewhere. These also break up the large public spaces and relieve the monotony which a concrete path or roadway brings. The tarmac roadways only lie in a narrow ribbon in certain restricted central areas. The constant battle between through traffic and the pedestrian and bicycle is more often won in Cambridge than in Oxford, where busy roads bisect the great city centre.

*

Old English cities are different from most of those on the Continent. A wall, crowded with houses, synonymous with 'civility', surrounds many old continental cities. Civilization is the city, an oasis in a landscape of peasants, ignorance and hard manual work. Think of Florence, Siena, Paris or Madrid.

Historically English cities have been different. They seem to have something of the countryside in them, just as the countryside has a feeling of the urban way of life. Norwich was described as 'a city in a garden or a garden in a city', a place where nature and culture blend together in avenues of trees, large parks and wild areas, the cult of the garden and the vegetable allotment. The English middle classes yearned for the cottage in the countryside and the power base of the upper middle class was the country house.

I remember being visited by a French journalist and academic who was amused and perhaps a little shocked to find me living 'like a peasant' in a thatched cottage in a large garden filled with trees and vegetables six miles outside Cambridge. No self-respecting French academic, he told me, would be seen dead in such a place. They like to live high up in a modern tower block in central Paris. They might escape to pseudo-peasant bucolic frolics for a month in August, like the English gentry escaping to the grouse moors, but their home was in the city.

Cambridge is a city in a garden, or a garden in a city. The central water meadows are filled with as much open grass and trees as with buildings. These are supplemented by the College Gardens, both along the Backs and in the centre of the city. Parallel to this are areas like Parker's Piece, the Botanical Gardens and a number of parks.

So the city is like a country estate; there is the main hall or house, but around it a highly controlled landscape laid out to delight.

Symbolically a fine chestnut stands at the very key point of the whole geography of Cambridge, between King's Chapel and the elegant Senate House. This tree, like the wonderful Japanese cherry at the back entrance to King's and many other trees in Cambridge, is protected. Not a bough can be cut without extensive negotiations with the planning department, for they are listed antiquities, like the buildings and manuscripts.

Indeed, many of the trees have known histories. A party in 2002 celebrated the two-hundredth birthday of an oriental plane tree which Edward Daniel Clark (subsequently the first Cambridge Professor of Mineralogy) had brought back from Thermopylae and planted in Christ's College Garden in 1802.[2] A mere youngster

Horse Chestnut and Senate House

If there is a centre to Cambridge it is this magnificent horse chestnut tree which stands between the religious centres, King's Chapel and St Mary's Church and the political and administrative centres, the Senate House, to the right in the picture, and the Old Schools.
[Photograph: courtesy Zhiguang Yin]

[2] As described in Martin Garrett, *Cambridge* (Oxford, 2004), 179; Peter Burke tells me that there is a similar huge oriental plane tree of about the same date in Emmanuel.

compared to the ancient mulberry supposedly planted by John Milton in the early seventeenth century in the same garden.

The willow and the majestic beech at King's Bridge symbolize the intersection between the past and present, nature and culture, England and the world. By half hiding the buildings as one approaches the bridge they add mystery to the old world beyond, curving lines framing the straight lines of Gibbs and the Chapel.

*

Cambridge is not just filled with colours and shapes but also with sound and silence. The music, the church bells, open-air madrigals on the river, pop bands at the May Balls, and above all the College choirs are part of the enchantment. From the start, the fact that the Colleges were based round religious services filled with plainchant and ancient music meant that university life was punctuated by music. The fact that the College Halls and particularly the Chapels provide a wonderful place for performances means that there has been a thread of music running through the eight hundred years of Cambridge history.

The presence of two choir schools, King's and St John's, of many music scholarships and more recently of a magnificent concert hall with its own gamelan instruments, bi-annual performances of Handel, and many concerts from Mongolian over-tone singing to Indian sitar music, gives a variety and richness to the musical scene.

To this we can add the world-famous Cambridge folk festival, the numerous musical events from aged rock bands to Chinese New Year celebrations in the Corn Exchange or the Junction. Then there are the annual musical events such as the Gilbert and Sullivan operas, jazz concerts on Jesus Green and a host of music societies.

All of this is symbolized and brought to a climax each Christmas for me by the carol services from King's where the choir in their scarlet and white robes send their voices up through the candle light into the dim vaults of the echoing ceiling. As I sit preparing myself for the mysterious Advent service, followed by the filming and recording of the service by the BBC to be seen and heard by millions around the world, my mind marvels at how all this seems so quintessentially English.

By chance I heard the service being broadcast when I was high up in the Himalayas in 1969, homesick for England and opening a packet of dried soup and half a bar of Cadbury's chocolate to celebrate Christmas. I never imagined that I would one day have the privilege of spending over thirty years a few yards from this great Chapel. I did not anticipate how this music would take me back to my childhood Christmas carols. But now, like many, I feel that in this conflict-torn world, the triumphant Christmas carols knit together past and present, obliterating time, raising us to a higher place.

It seems likely that music has seeped into the consciousness of most of those who have lived and worked in Cambridge, soothing or exciting, but always contributing to the way they think and feel. That the medieval carols, often with archaic words but with harmonies and melodies which still touch our hearts, should have remained so constant, yet ever changing, is another example of that blend of past and present which is so distinctive about Cambridge.

In between the music and the sound of bells and wind, there are the moments of contrasted stillness. With traffic just about kept at bay, there is still silence in Cambridge. There is the silence of still Quaker meetings, of misty mornings with punts gliding down the Cam, of the sun breaking through the stained glass windows in an empty Chapel.

*

Sitting in the almost dark Chapel last night as the candles lit up the red and white of the choir boys during the Advent Carol Service I realized that this marvellous building deserves a section on its own.

The Chapel, begun in 1446 and added to ever since, is a symbol of Cambridge. Each of its thin pillars can be seen as one branch of the academic traditions—history, mathematics, philosophy, and physics. The pillars soar upwards and then join in the fanned roof where all the human efforts to understand our world feed into each other and come to rest. It is a seamless and perfect resolution of disparate pressures. Like much of Cambridge, the Chapel is very old, yet it also feels as if it is young, fresh, clean and vigorous.

Between these threads of stone are the equally extraordinary windows, based on the great art of the Renaissance, and filled with deep colour, staining the white radiance of eternity, as Shelley might have put it. The imperfections in the glass hold the light and refract it so that the colours glow in a peculiar way. When the afternoon sun falls through them the stone is stained by the multi-coloured light.

The great Renaissance wooden screen where the angels fly on the top of the golden organ pipes is the finest example of such work north of the Alps and perhaps in the world. The woodwork of the stalls behind the choir is also superb.

William Wordsworth

William Wordsworth studied in Cambridge between 1787 and 1791. He was one of the many English poets educated in the University, from Spenser, Donne, Milton and Dryden, through Coleridge, Byron and Tennyson up to Rupert Brooke, Ted Hughes and Sylvia Plath. He represents the flourishing of the arts and humanities within the University.

There is much poetry and prose that celebrates the Chapel, but quoting too much of it, I have discovered, can cause irritation to those who have experienced many other beautiful chapels in Cambridge. So I shall be selective.

William Wordsworth wrote,

These lofty pillars, spread that branching roof
Self-poised, and scoop'd into ten thousand cells
Where light and shade repose, where music dwells
Lingering—and wandering on as loth to die;
Like thoughts whose very sweetness yieldeth proof
That they were born for immortality.

John Betjeman catches the mixture of colour and stone,

File into yellow candlelight, fair choristers of King's
Lost in shadowy silence of canopied stalls:
In blazing glass, above the dark, glow skies and thrones and wings
Blue, ruby, gold and green between the whiteness of the walls,
And with what rich precision the stonework soars and springs
To fountain out a spreading vault, a shower that never falls.

Even for non-believers the Chapel feels miraculous, a time and a space for transporting the spirit into other worlds. When the colours and shapes are added to the ethereal voices, drifting and echoing in the ways the poets describe, one almost feels as if the angels on the organ have come to life.

So the Chapel symbolizes and brings together the whole eight hundred years of efforts in Cambridge to go beyond this confused and corrupted world and to gaze into the depths and the heights, to see into the heart and soul of things. I feel overwhelmed by the privilege of living besides this great building, the windows of which were carefully taken apart, and stored during the Second World War, and then re-assembled. The bold outline against the ethereal blue sky or the tapestried windows on a cold winter's evening with the organ majestically playing is a constant delight.

*

Cambridge has preserved the past not only in its buildings, music and traditions, but as spirits. Cambridge is for me a place of ghosts. Sometimes I fancifully think this might be hereditary. My mother was a Rhodes James and a distant relative was the former Provost of King's and Eton, the antiquary and bibliographer Montague Rhodes James. He was also the most famous ghost story writer in the English language.

King's Night
King's College Chapel and the bridge at night, with the mysterious willow which probably features in Xu Zhimou's poem, 'On Saying Goodbye to Cambridge—Again'. It was on nights in King's that M.R. James read out his ghost stories to the assembled Fellows and walking across these lawns at night brings back many ghostly memories. [Photograph: courtesy Sean T. McHugh]

James's stories evoke misty nights, the echoes of emptiness, the howling winds, the rattling doors and windows of a Cambridge which still exists even with central heating and electricity. The oasis of good cheer and rationality amidst the encircling gloom, the beacon of scientific thought constantly threatened by physical and moral menace, which is one of the sub-themes of the stories, is something which resonates with Cambridge today.

James was writing at a time at the turn of the twentieth century when there was a widespread interest in trying to make contact with dead spirits through mediums. There was a lively Society for Psychical Research in the university which included among its members noted intellectuals, philosophers, economists and poets, including Henry Sidgwick, F.W.H. Myers, John Maynard Keynes and Rupert Brook. Gwen Raverat describes one colourful incident in this long and intriguing search for something beyond this material world. She describes how her uncle Frank, a son of Charles Darwin, along with Myers, was 'actually each holding an ankle of the medium Eusapia Palladino, when she made the movements which led to her exposure. This was unfortunate, for it shook the uncle's faith in all the subsequent investigations of the Society for Psychical Research.'[3]

Malcolm Lowry the novelist captures something of this eerie feeling when he describes the ancient courts at night seen through an alcoholic haze: 'fountains in moonlight and closed courts and cloisters, whose enduring beauty in its virtuous remote self-assurance, seemed part, less of the odd mosaic of one's stupid life there . . . . Than the strange dreams of some old monk, eight hundred years dead, whose forbidding house, reared upon piles and stakes driven into the marshy ground, had once shone like a beacon out of the mysterious silence, and solitude of the fens. A dream jealously

[3] Gwen Raverat, *Period Piece* (1952; paperback edition, 1987), 189. For a good account of psychical research in Cambridge by a contemporary, see Arthur Christopher Benson, *From a College Window* (1913), 286–8.

guarded: Keep off the Grass. And yet whose unearthly beauty compelled one to say: God forgive me'.[4]

*

The characteristic form of the ghost stories is the one behind most attempts to create a parallel world from Alice to Harry Potter. They start in normal, humdrum existence, a College room, a quiet evening at a country inn, and then something odd, or outré as another master of this genre, Edgar Allen Poe, would put it, occurs. A doll's house or picture comes alive, a tree seems to be infected with malignant things, and a room number 13 is there and then gone in the morning. This technique makes the hair on one's neck stand up, for we pass through a wardrobe, mirror, rabbit hole, passageway into a magic world filled with vague and menacing forces.

While all of this is deployed by James to create creepy stories, my own experience of Cambridge has given me the occasional feeling of falling through other rabbit holes. Here I find myself in parallel worlds of a less menacing kind, but where disbelief is temporarily suspended. These worlds are created by concentrated imagination and by piecing together parts of a lost encyclopedia like that described by Jorge Luis Borges. These are imagined worlds, not of ghosts, but of people living in other places I have studied as historian or anthropologist.

Of course all artists, writers and scientists create these imagined worlds, stray into fairyland, and then return to try to explain to others what they have experienced. What I have found special about Cambridge is that it allows many doors to open onto parallel worlds of enchantment. So, like many in Cambridge, I live all the time in several worlds. I can slip through a picture or book or, nowadays, an email or website, into other worlds and then come back again into the safe, encouraging, world of a Cambridge don.

*

[4]Quoted in Garrett, *Cambridge*, 100.

The second set of ghosts is of my former self. As I walk about Cambridge I keep meeting myself at other times and in different contexts. I cross King's Bridge and meet a younger self, lifting my children onto the parapet to watch the punts. I walk through King's garden and find myself thirty years earlier picking mushrooms on a now disappeared tennis court. I enter a smart new seminar room and find myself lecturing nervously from a different dais during my first days in Cambridge. I walk across the grass as the sky fills with stars above the Chapel roof and see myself ahead with my grandchildren waving red balloons in their party dresses. And, of course, annual events such as the Carol services or final parties on the lawns with the students bring back the ghosts of nearly forty years.

Such an experience occurs for everyone who has lived in one place for many years. I suspect it is especially powerful in Cambridge. The setting is so magnificent and each part is picked out so strongly that it becomes a living memory device for past experiences. If we add to this that many of the experiences were particularly powerful, and very often moments of delight, then it is not difficult to see how they are imprinted. Many of the pubs, lanes, fields, paths, rooms, chapels, and libraries are filled with my past ghostly self.

This is comforting, for while we grow old and our hair greys or falls out and the outside is wrinkled, the inner self, which feels no older, can meet its young reflections all around Cambridge. I assume that this is one of the pleasures for those who have studied at Cambridge. They come back after ten or twenty years and find it familiar and full of the ghosts of their vivid youth.

*

A third set of ghosts is of people I knew, or felt I knew, through their works if not in person. I feel a deep happiness in thinking that Spenser, Donne, Marvell and Milton or Wordsworth, Coleridge and Tennyson will have walked the very steps I am taking. As I tread where Francis Bacon, Newton, Darwin and Maxwell walked, I sense their physical presence as part of a long chain of thought.

There are also more recent ghosts. As I pass a certain road or house or College I think of people who I knew well and who have deeply influenced my work but who are now dead, historians, anthropologists or Fellows with whom I had a career changing conversation. Just as the University is a never-dying corporation or body, so it is filled with ghosts who never die. There used to be an old joke that when a good American died he went to Paris. Perhaps one could say that when a good Cambridge man (or woman) dies, she stays in Cambridge.

So the whole space, not just of King's, but also of the many Colleges and University, is electric with arguments, connections, sudden eureka moments. There are no plaques on any of the walls in these rooms. They are only selectively remembered along the corridors in old paintings and photographs. Yet their presence is an all-pervading atmosphere amongst the ghosts of Cambridge.

*

It is obviously impossible to quantify the effects of the physical environment of the University and College buildings of Cambridge on the minds of those who live in it, or were once students. It seems likely that it has been very considerable and I know from my own experience that there have been a number of times when the buildings and gardens have helped my mind and heart to soar beyond their usual confines.

John Stuart Mill the philosopher was convinced of the connection between elevation of feelings and ideas on the one hand, and spacious and charming environs on the other. 'Nothing contributes more to nourish elevation of sentiments in a people, than the large and free character of their inhabitations. The middle-age architecture, the baronial hall, and the spacious and lofty rooms, of this fine old place, so unlike the mean and cramped externals of English middle class life, gave the sentiment of a larger and freer existence, and were to me a sort of poetic cultivation . . . .'[5]

Vladimir Nabokov's explanation of why Cambridge had such an effect on him will lead us out into many of the themes in this book, for he puts it down specifically to the curious sense of time and memory in Cambridge. 'I know that I thought of Milton, and Marvell, and Marlowe, with more than a tourist's thrill as I passed beside the reverend walls. Nothing one looked at was shut off in terms of time, everything was a natural opening into it, so that one's mind grew accustomed to work in a particularly pure and ample environment, and because, in terms of space, the narrow lane, the cloistered lawn, the dark archway hampered one physically, that yielding diaphanous texture of time was, by contrast, especially welcome to the mind, just as a sea view from a window exhilarates one hugely, even though one does not care for sailing.'[6]

---

[5]John Stuart Mill, *Autobiography* (OUP World Classics edition, 1952), 47.
[6]Vladimir Nabokov, *Speak, Memory* (Penguin, 1967), 207.

CULTURE

Cambridge is a cloistered space. That is not to say that every College has a 'covered walk round a quadrangle or along the side of a convent or College or cathedral building', though many do have such a thing. It is more in the wider sense of being enclosed, 'shut up', 'immured' (within walls).

A wall, traditionally meant to be impenetrable to students or others wishing to climb in out of hours, surrounds each College. The spikes and broken glass and other fortifications which were so impressively attempting to guard the fortress have now been replaced by CCTV cameras watching out for thieves rather than undergraduates trying to enter or leave the College.

Yet it is not the actual physical enclosure that I want to emphasize, but the mixture of closedness with openness which is a feature of cloisters. Cloisters are half open, as are the social and mental cloisters which exist everywhere in Cambridge.

The great advantage of a cloister is that it is, in Gerry Martin's phrase, 'bounded but leaky'. It is bounded, protected, shut off from the heat of the sun on scorching days, or the drenching rain on others. Yet it is also 'leaky' or rather open; one can look out through the open, unglazed, side away from the main building. This gives the special feeling as in the marvellous cloisters in the back court of

Trinity or the old court at Queen's College. It is possible to walk, talk and think while being protected.

This is an allegory for Cambridge. It is a protected space, guarded by its wealth, prestige, meticulous organization, liberal atmosphere and its traditions. It has many protected cloisters of the mind and spirit. Yet it is not shut off. It is always possible to look out and receive impressions, fresh air and scents, movement and experience. It keeps the tension between inside and outside, private and public, secret and exposed. This cloistering effect, where people sense that they are within some half-private, half public space is but a small microcosm of something larger.

*

The need for such outdoor but sheltered walks partly arises from a realization that walking and thinking are deeply intertwined, as the Greeks knew with their idea of 'peripatetic philosophers'. I like to think of the motto *Solvitur ambulando*, 'it is solved by walking', or of Albert Einstein's remark that 'the legs are the wheels of creativity'. There are an infinite number of examples of the 'Eureka' moment occurring on a walk, alone or with friends. A famous picture of Crick and Watson shows them walking down the path behind King's College.

I think through the final version of my lectures as I walk round the beautiful Fellow's Garden at King's, or along the Backs on a clear morning as the lakes of crocuses shimmer under the ancient trees behind Trinity. Charles Darwin built a 'thinking path' through his estate at Down House where he paced endlessly trying to solve the great puzzle of his age after returning from Cambridge where he had examined and arranged his Beagle collections.

Kyoto with its magnificent shrines and temples is one city I have visited which I have found vies with Oxford and Cambridge for ancient beauty. It has developed its own 'philosopher's walk' along a small stream between the shrines and temples. In some ways it could be said that all of Cambridge is a 'philosopher's walk'. It is a city where

Charles Darwin

Charles Darwin studied in Cambridge between 1828 and 1831. Here he is aged 31 years old, four years after the voyage in the Beagle. He represents the many scientists who were taught or worked in Cambridge before the twentieth century, including William Harvey, Isaac Newton, Charles Babbage and James Clerk Maxwell. Darwin's theory of evolution through natural selection is a model for how Cambridge has developed over the last eight hundred years.

the Fellows and students, once they have reached the centre through the clogged arteries of traffic, can walk almost everywhere in under ten minutes. The place is on a tiny scale. By cutting through known routes and courts, it is possible to reach ninety percent of the Colleges and the University (with the exception of the new science site in the west) on foot without spending more than a minute or two on busy, car-infested, roads. When I first came to Cambridge I used to walk from my flat outside the College to my work place in my bedroom slippers without feeling conspicuous.

So Cambridge is a park with many buildings, gardens and special walks for all weathers and all states of mind. The centre is so concentrated that almost every walk leads to chance encounters with old friends and students. Although it is many times larger than the fenland village I now live in, I meet many more people I know and it feels more like a village. A nod, a wave of the hat, a smile, a quick chat, an agreement to meet for longer, all these occur several times a day.

I was told by a visually impaired student in my Department that her study of Cambridge pavements showed that they were very carefully partitioned, with pockets of resistance to her movement outside certain shops, different channels down which tourists moved, undergraduates rushed, and dons walked. An invisible set of criss-cross routes lies across the visible surface.

This is bound to happen in a relatively crowded space where people are moving about for different purposes, from the half-day Chinese tourist to the stooped figure of some elderly Fellow with his hands clasped behind his back. My first visit to Cambridge and King's was for a Conference in 1967. I was overwhelmed by the grandeur and charm. My memory is reinforced by long, deep, conversation-filled walks with some of my intellectual heroes of that time. I remember that first expression on the face of Cambridge, even as the place and I grow older.

So Cambridge, like each of us, goes through its cycle. Traces of its medieval youth, middle-aged self-confidence and autumn grandeur, all the ages in one, and all visible in tiny signs which can be discerned if one walks it constantly, looking at buildings from the back, from above and from the inside.

*

Cambridge is a large museum. It is an eight hundred year old collection of treasures of all kinds, paper, papyrus, parchment, cloth, glass, stone, ceramics, oil on canvas, wooden carvings, stone, trees and ancient dons. Whereas in most societies the old is thrown away, being of diminishing status as time passes, the English are reluctant to abandon things and they become more valued with age.

We may wonder why the English should be great collectors and preservers. Why do they go all around the world collecting other people's cast off objects, to display the great collections in the Archaeology and Anthropology Museum, the Fitzwilliam, the

Whipple and elsewhere? Why do they delight in telling people that a certain object is five hundred or five thousand years old, as if this antiquity gave it extra prestige?

Collecting is partly about pattern making. To be a professional collector of anything involves creating a mental map—of early ceramics, stamps, books or whatever is the theme of the collection—and then filling in the parts in detail. There is an obvious delight in encountering something new for the collection, in completing a 'set', whether of the twelve volumes of the *Golden Bough*, or a full set of interviews of the great chemists and molecular biologists who worked to piece together the pattern of DNA. Humans love jigsaws, crosswords, filling in gaps. What better hobby than to build up a fine library like Joseph Needham, or a collection of paintings like John Maynard Keynes, or a set of antique silver like Jack Plumb? Then, having built it up one gives the whole collection away to one's old College or someone who will treasure it.

Collecting is also a sociable activity. There are numerous clubs and small groups to compare notes on how far one has got, to organize expeditions to collect books, sightings of rare birds, rocks and minerals or whatever is the essence of the collection. As Orwell observed, 'We are a nation of flower-lovers, but also a nation of stamp-collectors, pigeon-fanciers, amateur carpenters, coupon-snippers, darts-players, cross-world-puzzle fans.'[1] The main requirement is enthusiasm and a growing expertise, some money, some space. Cambridge Colleges, libraries and museums give more space for the retention of the old than can be found in most parts of the world, and allow this mania to be pursued. The ingenuity of the classification and storage of the materials is not dissimilar to the ingenuity needed to classify and store facts and theories in professional fields of work. As new technologies of inspecting and analysing these collections emerge they are constantly being re-interpreted and refreshed.

[1] George Orwell, *The Lion and the Unicorn* (Penguin edition, 1982), 39.

Such collecting hobbies ease social relations. The English—and many Cambridge dons are an extreme case—often face the problem of what to talk about after the inevitable topics of the weather, sport and the uselessness of the current government have been exhausted. When I meet a fellow collector, whatever his or her background, there is a moment of closeness. The passion, which started in the collecting and exchanging of symbolic valuables at my preparatory school, marbles, venerable conkers, or white mice, never dies and one continues to compare, swop, admire their adult equivalents with equal zeal.

*

Cambridge is both sage and filled with child-like enthusiasms. The first reason for the youthful feeling comes from one of the main roles of English universities. As a Venetian Ambassador noticed in the fifteenth century, the English are peculiar in that rather than keeping their children at home until they are adult, they send them away to be brought up by people other than their own family. In the period of which he wrote, if they were poor they were sent out to other families as servants or apprentices, often from the age of seven. If they were middle class or above they were sent as young serving persons or courtiers to the houses of rich acquaintances, or to Oxford and Cambridge.

Oxford and Cambridge, which at that time took undergraduates at a much younger age (from fourteen or fifteen onwards) were boarding institutions for young boys who moved through their adolescence into early adulthood at university. It was here that the child becomes the man. Through this 'rite of transition', a young person emerged ready for the world of adult responsibilities. It was often a period of freedom and liminality, of separation from the world in order to make it possible to re-enter it with a different status. The Colleges acted *in loco parentis*, in the place of parents. They still see themselves as doing this nowadays.

This is such an obvious function of Cambridge today that it is easy not to notice it. There are rites of incorporation at the start, a period of liminality and licence with inculcation into new knowledge in the middle, and a rite of dis-aggregation at the end (degree ceremonies etc). This gives the basic structure to the undergraduate course. There is a first year of innocence, a second of gaining knowledge, a third of 'finals' which ties it all together before the nostalgically remembered 'Salad Days' are over.

This central feature of ritual and social transition is now partly concealed by the growing number of postgraduates and the movement of the age of undergraduates from 14–17 to 18–21 over the eighteenth and nineteenth centuries. Those who come up are already in many ways sophisticated and mature. Yet they are still on the cusp between adolescence and maturity and this gives Cambridge its special youthful feeling. Over half of the University population are aged 18–21, full of a mixture of innocence, nearness to childhood, enthusiasm, open futures, exploring minds. This seeps into the soul of even the crabbiest old don who each year partly relives his or her own years as a hopeful young monster. As my friend Peter Burke puts it, 'I have experienced a sense of temporary rejuvenation every October for more than 40 years, including the sense of a clean slate, the opportunity not to make the mistakes of the year before.'

The jokes, pranks, satires, spirited life of the bar, the disco, the Union, the clubs and societies are all related to this period of testing, trying and expanding. The hobbies and interests at school can now be broadened, the first solo journeys to foreign lands undertaken. New passions for ideas, and perhaps the first serious love affairs can blossom.

The theme of childhood continues in another peculiar feature which visitors noted, namely that the English never want to grow old and indeed succeeded to some extent in remaining child-like. As Emile Cammaerts, a Belgian author who settled in England in 1908, observed, 'This unwillingness to grow old is an essential feature of the English folklore of the twentieth century. When the learned scientists of the future endeavour to trace the origin of the Peter Pan myth, as no doubt they will, they will be obliged to recognize that it is peculiar to this island.'[2]

Many of those I have interviewed continue to ask the childish questions when grown up—the big 'why' questions. As soon as wonder, astonishment and the famous curiosity of children disappears, the mind grows dull and unproductive. The great Cambridge thinkers, who have penetrated to the edges of time and the universe, or deep to the basic sub-atoms and genes of life, continue to ask these questions. They do not become blasé. They know how little they know.

The lives of a number of very distinguished intellectuals have often been rather unsuccessful for long periods, often poorly paid and frustrating, yet they have persevered out of curiosity and wonder. They have engaged in an ambitious attempt to understand certain mysteries of the world in the knowledge that they will never know the full answer, but that perhaps a new part or secret will be discovered.

*

The challenges of the mind are echoed in the challenges of the body. Foreigners visiting Oxford and Cambridge in the nineteenth century were amazed at the huge emphasis on competitive games and sports in the life of the two universities. The 'boat race between Oxford and Cambridge and the inter-university cricket matches had already begun as early as 1827, and became annual events in 1839.'[3] Boat clubs and other athletic organizations and inter-collegiate competitions became a well established feature of the University. The emphasis on sports was a continuation of what was happening in the public schools and helped to bridge the transition from school to university.

[2]Cammaerts in Francesca M. Wilson (ed.), *Strange Island* (1955), 252.
[3]History of the University, on the University website.

The Cambridge University Diary includes the year's almanac, examination timetable, university officers, libraries, museums, Colleges and other matters in a few pages. It then devotes two pages to 'The River' with the 'Order of Boats in the Main Division'. Then a further two pages are given to 'Inter-University' contests, one third of which are 'Women's Matches'. There are thirteen 'Full Blue' sports, and another twenty-six 'Discretionary' and 'Half Blue Sports', including Judo, Karate, Water Polo, Fives (Eton), Fives (Rugby), Korfball, Pistol Shooting and Table Tennis. The Women's Matches include Football, Judo, Orienteering and Rugby Football.

Perhaps the concern with games and sports is not quite as great as twenty years ago, when the examination pressures were less, yet it is clear that a huge amount of the time and energy of the students, and of the many senior members who coach and support them, is given to sport. Many English sportsmen developed their skills at university and the first unified 'Cambridge rules' of football were devised there in the middle of the nineteenth century. Having played football for my Oxford College, and before that devoted up to a quarter of my school life at the Dragon and Sedbergh to competitive sports, I would be an odd anthropologist not to wonder why games are so central to British education.

Several theories spring to mind. There is the old adage 'a sound mind in a sound body'. That is to say, if one's body is clean and lean, your mind will work better. This is certainly part of what drove me out onto wet, cold and muddy fields. This fitness is not just the muscular exercise, which relaxes and tones up the body, but the relaxation of the mind.

In a university one is under constant mental pressure, writing the next essay in one's dreams and all waking hours. Something rather powerful is needed to clear the mind. The Japanese have Zen and the tea ceremony. Alcohol or chess can help. Yet it has often struck me that rowing along a misty river in perfect unison early in the morning as the sun rises over the willow trees or being involved in executing complex moves in a game of football or rugby has a similar effect. It is difficult to think of a problem in physics or history in the midst of a rugby scrum.

Cricket, however, is a puzzle. The long periods of inactivity waiting to bat, or fielding in some remote position, should give one ample time to fret over intellectual matters. Strangely, however, playing cricket seems to suspend thought, to put one into a sort of trance, out of time and space. As one wit quipped, the English, not being a religious people, invented cricket to give themselves a sense of eternity.

I was told at school that games were important because they taught me lessons for life. Team games both expressed and gave instruction in three things which would stand me in good stead well beyond the particular game. The first was that while the action was proceeding in its bounded arena, the game was all that mattered. I should play as hard as possible, try to win, struggle and strive. Yet, in the end it is the journey, not the outcome, that matters. I was to learn that whatever the game, including larger games like local or national politics or any other competitive situation in life, I should remember that a game is only a game. The arguments in the House of Commons, the battles I was to fight in my Faculty or College, or the contested actions in courts of law, all these are similar to games. I should take them seriously while they lasted, then laugh and shake hands whatever the outcome. A good loser was as admirable as a good winner.

This gives an odd flavour to much English political life, from the micro level of student or University politics, up to the House of Commons, where the cricket analogy is often employed. The point is well made by Tocqueville. 'No people carry so far, especially when speaking in public, violence of language, outrageousness of theories, and extravagance in the inferences drawn from those theories. Thus your A.B. says, that the Irish have not shot half enough landlords. Yet no people act with more moderation. A quarter of what is said in England at a public meeting, or even round a dinner table, without anything being done or intended to be done, would in France announce violence, which would almost always be more furious than the language had been'.[4]

The second lesson is that we have to play by the rules. Rules are general and minimal and the art is to steer as close to their edge as possible, without breaking them. One should pass the ball *almost* forwards, tackle with energy and skill but *not* trip up deliberately, sail as close to the wind literally and metaphorically as possible. Yet one should never cheat, even if no one could see. Victory by cheating is pointless for you were entrusted to play the game by the rules.

This lesson should apply if you became a lawyer, a politician, a civil servant, a churchman, a banker, an academic or any other middle class professional. Most behaviour is partly competitive and much of it occurs out of sight and cannot be scrutinized. Others trust you to play cleanly. On the playing fields and games courts which surround Cambridge, people learn, as they had to at school, that cheating does not pay, not because you may be penalized, but because you lose your own self-esteem and this subverts the whole point of the game.

The third lesson was that team games improved teamwork skills. It has often been noticed that most of the world team games— including cricket, football, and rugby—were developed in England. And at the heart of these activities, as with rowing, playing in an orchestra or singing in a choir, it is the general good, the team's success, that matters.

The art is to achieve a balance between individual initiative and effort—pulling the oar, dribbling the ball—and the needs of the larger whole. To pull too strongly, to hold onto the ball too long, can destroy the team effort. The activity is largely about collaboration, about depending on others and others depending on you. Thus 'a good team player' is one of the higher forms of praise for a member of a College or Department.

[4]Alexis de Tocqueville, *Memoir, Letters, and Remains of Alexis de Tocqueville* (Cambridge, 1961), II, 353.

The impressive record of many units of the British armed forces, or of the laboratories and business firms, are linked to this involvement in team activities. Golf, chess, shooting and fishing, of course, teach different skills. Muscular academia, a continuation of muscular schooling, which I both loved and wearied of in the end, is an important thread of Cambridge life.

The inter-College and inter-university rivalries, are a perfect setting for team sports as 'Houses' were at school. It may not be true that the battle of Waterloo was won on the playing fields of Eton, yet it is clear that if suddenly all sports and games were banned in universities a great deal of the meaning and sparkle would be lost, and the role of these institutions would be diminished. Games are not just a luxury; they are part of the fabric.

The University, its Departments and Colleges, can be seen as involved in one long game, a game to discover the meaning and secrets of the Universe and of human life here on earth. Teams of thinkers, who compete and collaborate over the centuries, play that game. It is a huge game, as Francis Crick indicated in the title of his book *What Mad Pursuit*. It cannot be played alone. Even Newton was part of a huge scientific team stretching over Europe and beyond.

Rose and Ziman suggest that 'Oxbridge research has a style of its own—a style that is recognisable as its special contribution to the world of the mind. It is an aristocratic style, self-confident, alert, and elegant. To the best Oxford and Cambridge scholar, research is not a labour, nor a duty—it is a game. The final results may not matter so much as the manner in which they are achieved and expounded. The era of sealing wax and string is over— but the principle that it embodies, the making of beautiful discoveries with the slenderest means, is still part of the ethos of the Oxbridge scientist.'[5]

In Cambridge, as in life, there is not a rigid division between thinking and doing, between the mind and the body, the individual

[5]Rose and Ziman, *Camford Observed*, 222.

and the group. As John Donne put it, 'No man is an island . . . .' And so when the flag flies over King's College, as it is doing today for one of my colleagues who tragically died young after a game of squash, I feel diminished. One notable player in the team is gone. But the game must and will go on.

*

What one eats, the manner of eating, and with whom one shares a meal are important class markers in any society. They are particularly important in Cambridge for several reasons.

Crème Brulée, a burnt custard supposedly accidentally discovered in Trinity College, Cambridge in the eighteenth century, is often served at the end of a special dinner. By that time a mellow glow has usually descended on the guests, well fortified with choice wines and foods. As a College choir sings madrigals and the Head of House makes a toast to the new Fellows, honoured guests, the pious founder or to 'The College', the effervescent feeling of being slightly out of this world takes one over. The occasion creates a sense of 'community', of being linked to others at a bodily and spiritual level. Eating and drinking together is to feel as one, to share a table in the spirit of 'commensality'.

Along with the chapel, the largest and most splendid buildings in the Colleges are the dining halls. Cleanliness may come close to godliness, but it could also be said that consumption is close to devotion. Like Chinese ancestor halls, these buildings are hung with portraits of 'ancestors'. The ceremonials and socializing which occur both express and create much of the special atmosphere for those who pass through Cambridge.

I was somewhat prepared for this emphasis on communal eating by a boarding school where we sat on long wooden benches. There we supposedly learnt how to hold our knives and forks, how to show politeness to our neighbours and engage in sociable conversations. Later I heard that the ability to eat politely—how to eat peas without causing chaos—was supposed to be a major hurdle for getting a Cambridge Fellowship.

Previously, with a small Fellowship, one would have known other Fellows very well. Now, in my College at least, it is too big to have this pleasure, and I find the randomness of having to sit next to strangers somewhat disconcerting. Yet I do understand how eating together is a central expression of 'Fellowship'. From the sacredness of the Holy Communion where believers eat the bread and drink the wine together, through to the rowdiest boat club dinner, the sharing of food expresses a form of unity. The highest mark of intimacy an English family can show is to invite you into their home for a meal, especially on special occasions like a birthday or Christmas.

It has always struck me as odd that 'eating your dinners' is an essential part of becoming qualified as a barrister at the Inns of Court. Yet it does make sense, since sitting side by side and eating and being able to converse widely on many subjects are essential features of that widespread view that a co-operative, collaborative sort of spirit is absolutely necessary for success.

*

Visitors noted that the English were great eaters, even if they might not have been great chefs. From the start of Cambridge University eight hundred years ago, the unusual wealth and productivity of English agriculture meant that most people in England were unusually well fed compared to their neighbours. Whereas the mass of people throughout the world until the later nineteenth century were dependent on a largely subsistence diet, mainly of inferior grains and vegetables, in England it was different. There was wheat and plentiful barley for beer, a large pastoral sector provided excellent beef, mutton, pork and other meats. The rivers and surrounding sea supplied a wide range of fish and the dairy industry provided ample butter and cheese.

The already unusually high quality of the raw foodstuffs off which Cambridge dons and students fed from the thirteenth century onwards was given another boost in the eighteenth century. One of the most important agricultural revolutions in history occurred in the neighbouring counties of Suffolk and Norfolk. In this process, the great fields were farmed in a new way using clover and root crops, particularly turnips. The new methods both rested and restored the soil's richness. It also made it possible to feed the stalled animals through the winter, providing an even better supply of meat and milk products for the Cambridge dining tables and manure for further invigorating the fields.

The tables of the Cambridge Colleges were not just filled with local produce from their East Anglian farms. There was beef from Scotland, cheeses from Wales and Cornwall, wine from France and Italy. This was because the city of Cambridge was the hub of one of the greatest distribution systems in Europe. Fairs grew up all over Europe in the Middle Ages and there were very notable ones in Germany, France and Spain. Yet by the later seventeenth century, helped by long peace and the excellent water transport from the sea up the Ouse and then the Cam, the largest fair in Europe was at Stourbridge, on the edge of Cambridge.

The ghost of this fair remains long after the railways and the roads undermined its formal existence. In Cheddar (cheese) Lane, Garlic Row and the pub signs on the Newmarket road (the Wrestlers pub, the sign with the seven stars of the Earl of Oxford), and the small Norman building by the railway bridge, once a plague chapel and then a store house for the fair, there are signs of what was once there. When Daniel Defoe in the early eighteenth century devoted more pages to his description of the fair than to the University, Stourbridge was an exchange market for the wealth of Western Europe from the Baltic through the central continent down to the Mediterranean.

Cambridge University includes a 'corporate entertainment business' where many organizations have their 'bonding' sessions amidst the splendour and sumptuous wines and foods. Yet it also remains a place where food is one of the central unifiers for students and dons, whether in the magnificence of dining halls or in the increasing wealth of cosmopolitan restaurants.

'We are what we eat' is a well-known saying. Thought of in this way, many of those who have passed through the University and Colleges have often had a privileged gastronomic experience in the most congenial of surroundings. As the Fellows retire from the great candle-lit halls to the portrait-filled and often panelled wine rooms, where the port trundles round on a little silver train-like contraption and the silver snuffboxes are ceremonially placed on the table, I feel part of some timeless world. While all this eating and drinking sometimes seems excessive and antique, and carried to excess it is ridiculous, it does draw together people who are normally shut away in their private and individual minds and disciplines.

THE CULTURE OF POLITICS

In his book *Homo Ludens* the historian Johan Huizinga shows that humans are playful creatures, full of imagination, competitiveness and a desire to experiment. Play can be 'deep', as in the analysis of the cockfight in Bali by Clifford Geertz, or at a surface level. It can have serious or trivial ends, and it can encompass many fields including politics, law, art and science. Looking at Cambridge as an arena for playful activity in the widest sense helps us to enter one of its most intriguing and characteristic features.

One of the team 'games' in Cambridge is local politics, often based on small factions. The local politics of the dons is mirrored among students, some of whom start to practice for the world of Westminster politics in the Cambridge Union Society, with its confrontational debates, or in the numerous other debating societies and political clubs. There are a number of factors which make university politics into a particularly complex game, like multi-dimensional chess. One is the nature of the players. Many of the dons are by training experts in the art of argument.

The fact that many dons have multi-stranded relationships to each other, that secrecy and alliances are frequently necessary, that your enemies' enemy is often your friend, that your friend on one occasion is your enemy on another, all adds to the intensity and amount of this activity.

Recently in an interview, the retired head of a big Department who was also the head of a College expressed wonder at the way in which the Department meeting was businesslike and quick in the morning, and the College meeting might go on for hours in the afternoon. This is what you would expect, for the College is in some ways like a large family, while the Department is more like a business.

All of the politicking rises to a crescendo when an important post, particularly a Mastership of a College, is to be filled. The world depicted in C.P. Snow's *The Masters* is one I have experienced in four Provostship elections in Cambridge. Each of these occupied the seventy or so active Fellows for many hundreds of hours. The factions, feuds, vendettas, deals, uncertainties are very elaborate.

It does not take a great stretch of imagination to realize that it is this form of competitive politicking, especially over recruitment and honours, like the fusion through feuding described by anthropologists, that holds the Colleges together. It is during electoral battles, as well as during debates on contentious decisions on matters of principle, major expenditure or a large change such as the admission of women, that a College really comes alive. It is then that one has something meaningful and shared to talk about to colleagues, many of whom inhabit worlds about which one knows too little to carry on a more than desultory conversation without some College 'business' to discuss.

It is in these periods of heightened emotion and apparently critical decisions that the structural tensions within a group of people become more visible. The study of national and global politics has been enriched for many by their practical involvement in these local politics. Certainly I had never felt much interest in political history or political philosophy until I began to be caught up on the edges of university and College politics. Much of it is like tribal politics in egalitarian societies. There are long arguments, veiled threats and pressures, but, in the end, only if a person wins a consensus and the respect of his or her fellows, can they achieve much. This is because there is very little formal, instituted, power. The Head of a College or Department can exert no physical force and has limited power of hiring and firing. The system depends on a certain amount of charisma and respect within an old structure.

*

I still remember my panic when I first took on Committee responsibilities in Cambridge as a member of the daunting 'Fellowship Electors' at King's with its Nobel Prize winners, unfamiliar oaths and rituals. I was more or less tongue-tied for three years. Becoming Academic Secretary of a Faculty Board after only nine months in the Department was equally daunting.

Coming straight out of pure research, I had no idea of how to take minutes, how to organize an agenda, when one should vote, what fell into reserved business, on how to lobby people. The whole ethos and nature of committees, which seemed so important as a way of running Cambridge, was a black fog. No one really ever explained to me either how committees work or how the committees I was on fitted within the wider administrative organization.

Gradually, over the years, this has changed. Through attending over two hundred and fifty Faculty Boards and Degree Committees, over five hundred Department meetings and Examiner's meetings, and over two hundred other University Committees, and hundreds of College Committees, I began to glimpse how they seemed to work.

I learnt how to find a middle way between fiercely opposed arguments, how to 'kick into touch' difficult issues which people would usually soon forget about, how to persuade people of the value and dangers of an approach. I learnt how to 'fix' things—when appropriate and possible—before a meeting, how to keep good relations with people higher up in the administration and how to work closely with the secretaries.

I cannot say that I exactly enjoyed most of the hundreds of hours of my life I have spent sitting on Committees. Yet I have savoured the pleasures of good-natured and honest discussion, efficient and fair execution of business, and the generally consensual and rational nature of most of the meetings. This pleasure grew with my greater understanding of the way in which what I was doing fitted into the larger structure of Cambridge.

I came to appreciate the final verdict of Cornford. 'But if you find that I was right, remember that other world, within the microcosm, the silent, reasonable world, where the only action is thought, and thought is free from fear. If you go back to it now . . . you will find yourself in the best of all company—the company of clean, humorous, intellect; and if you have a spark of imagination, and try very hard to remember what it was like to be young, there is no reason why your brains should ever get woolly, or anyone should wish you out of the way. Farewell!'[1]

The main thing I learned was that the key players were at the bottom of the hierarchy, the largely independent and self-motivated academic staff, whose agreement to any change was essential. Although it is changing rapidly, Cambridge is still basically a bottom-up system of power which is both unusual and under constant threat. It is still one where any University Teaching Officer can strongly affect the whole business of the University. In their hands lies the vitality and innovation of the institution.

*

The ordinary members of Departments come together weekly in term. These are the essential building blocks of the University and the power of the Departments has been maintained over my time in Cambridge and indeed recently reinforced in my Faculty.

The Departments are then sometimes grouped into a higher level, in my case the three Departments of Archaeology, Anthropology and Biological Anthropology form one Faculty. The Faculty for a long period was active as a mediator between Departments, but its

[1]Cornford, reprinted in Johnson, *University Politics*, 110.

power has tended to drift either upwards, to the increasingly powerful 'Schools', or downwards to the Department. It was never much more than an administrative arrangement, very often without a real community life.

The Schools themselves then funnel decisions up and down from the general executive committee, the General Board of the University chaired by the Vice Chancellor. Of the higher levels— of the Regent House, of the powerful university committees—many dons, including myself, have little experience. Yet we have traditionally had confidence in their rather light regulation since we vote for the members and usually know one or two of them as friends and colleagues. Only once or twice have I attended debates on specific issues or lobbied these higher committees.

Basically the University is a branching structure. It is based on the feudal model with the King, barons, gentry, manor, village and individual. It can be likened to an army. Each rank has its functions and competes with units at its level, but it also joins with similar-level units in opposition to more distant outsiders. People rise to the limit of their competence and interest for a time, but power is slippery. Establishing a dictatorship in such a system is impossible. It is, as far as any administrative organization of this size can be, a working democracy or 'aristo-democracy' as Cornford called it.

*

'All power tends to corrupt; absolute power corrupts absolutely.' As the Cambridge historian Lord Acton knew when he coined this aphorism, his University was no exception. In any institution, as in any game, there are many grey and ambiguous zones, conflicts of interests, contradictory pressures, which mean that there is a fine and almost invisible line between honest, scrupulous behaviour, and a bending of the rules.

This is especially likely where, as in Cambridge, so many relationships overlap. It is often difficult to know where friendship ends and favouritism begins, where an interest should be declared before a decision is made, where supporting a student becomes patronage, or where an implicit deal is being done for the exchange of advantages. Let me give two examples.

When dealing with University and College admissions, it can be argued that if one is faced with two roughly equal candidates it would be absurd not to use all the information available to one, including past form, schooling and family. Others would regard this as corruption, distorting the admissions process. Certainly great efforts are being made to achieve balance. For example, one of the most direct links, which meant that up to a century and a half ago only students from Eton could go to King's, has changed to the present situation where three quarters of King's students come from the State sector.

The conflicts of interests tend to grow as a person gains seniority. I have often found myself wearing several 'hats' at the same time. As a member of a Department I feel every part of the proposed budget is needed by the Department, but as Chair of the Library Committee I should push the case for a larger donation to the book fund, while as a Fellow of a rich College, it might be more useful for spare money to be spent on a fund to help with teaching in poorer Colleges.

There are various devices to try to minimize such conflicts. A person should declare for whom he or she is speaking—'Putting on my Library Hat . . . .' They should declare interests or remain silent because of them. For example, in my Department by convention a supervisor of a Ph.D. student takes no part in the discussion and appointment of the internal examiner for that student. When a person's request for leave of absence or membership of an important committee is being discussed, they are asked to leave the room.

Before I understood what was happening, I found this last device undermining. Why was I being sent out? Were there secret things I had done which needed to be aired? Was I thought to be too prejudiced to be able to enter into the discussion? If the leave or committee membership were denied I would never know what the cause was.

Later, having sat through many of the discussions of others, I realized that it was not a time for character assassination or gossip. Rather it made it possible for people to say what they honestly felt without creating enmities, or the embarrassing sight of a person pleading his or her own cause.

Of course these procedures, and in particular the numerous 'fire walls' or invisible protective barriers, depend almost entirely on a code of honour and of keeping to one's promises. To speak frankly and openly in a meeting which is meant to be secret, and then to hear that everything has been leaked to the subject of the discussion does happen, but fortunately not often. For most people, most of the time, loyalty to the institution and to the general good comes before narrow self-interest or personal friendships.

As far as I have observed, there is little gross corruption, that is the buying of favours, the perverting of donor's intentions, the selling of degrees or wine cellars. No one has ever offered me money or favours to alter their exam marks, or to give their children an entrance place. I have scarcely ever sensed undue favouritism or personal self-interest corrupting the proceedings.

Indeed, it is one of the great pleasures of working in Cambridge that by expecting the highest standards of ethical behaviour, despite quite large potential rewards for cutting corners, most people live up to the expectations. There are secret scandals and corruptions and they occasionally become public. Yet I have never encountered a single person who has been openly accused, tried and expelled for corrupt behaviour involving money or favours. This is quite an achievement in a place where power may not be absolute, but there is a good deal of wealth and prestige to be fought over.

RHYTHMS

It is often thought that one of the main changes in the last couple of hundred years, linked to the rise of industrial societies, is that time has flattened out. It flies like an arrow and never returns to its point of origin, it is progressive and linear.

This is in contrast with time in agricultural societies which is thought of as circular, linked to the seasons, to the sowing, growth and harvesting of plants and the movement of herds. There are mushrooms—it must be autumn; a time to plant, a time to weed, a time to reap, then a time to plant again.

One of the curious features of a University is that it maintains, within one of the most rationalized and highly technical parts of a society, a circular rhythm. There are four seasons printed in my Cambridge diary.

'Michaelmas', is the late autumn and Christmas, the time of entry of the fresh batch of students and the starting of lectures. It is a time to sow. The 'Lent' term is the hard slog through the cold spring, the consolidation of teaching. This is the time of vigorous weeding and tending of growing minds. Then there is the 'Easter' term, that is the spring and early summer. This is the revision and examination season, the rounding off of many courses. It is the harvesting and laying in of the harvest, and the harvest festivals (May Balls, graduations) and the saying good-bye.

Finally there is the Summer Vacation, or as it was renamed recently in the diary to cloud the eyes of suspicious accountants, the 'Summer Research Period'. This is the time for family and recovery from a demanding year. It is also the time for deeper research, writing and foreign trips. It is a mixture of preparing the ground, sorting out the seed for new teaching, long-term projects to reshape the whole terrain and widening one's social and mental worlds. The cycle is complete and starts over again, thirty-five times in my life as a teacher.

On top of this there are the three-year cycles of an undergraduate or a Ph.D. course, a beginning, middle and year end. In the case of a Ph.D. this is often thought of as preparation, gathering the data or doing the experiments and 'writing up'. With undergraduates it is first year, second year and Finals.

These cycles are mirrored in nature. Because Cambridge is filled with flowers, lawns and above all trees, the academic cycle is linked to the movement of the leaves and grasses. In particular in spring I watch out for the slight haze of green of the willows on the Backs. I relish the first aconites and then the bluebells, the daffodils, the crocuses, and later the red tulips under the white cherry blossoms. Full summer brings a green luxuriance. This later turns to red and gold and is blown away by the winter gales.

As the days shorten and then lengthen, the shadows on the buildings and the changing light makes the whole place like a great sundial. It reflects in its whole architecture the actual antique sundials which one suddenly notices above the entrance to King's Chapel or on a seventeenth century side gate into Caius.

This circular, living, time, alleviates boredom. Cambridge is not a static and stale place, but rather I feel movement, change, and an ever-refreshing renewal here. Yet also there is the assurance of continuity, of a safe return, of predictability.

*

The other unusual feature is that space is close to pre-industrial space. In the village in Nepal which I have often visited for my anthropological fieldwork, each part of the village and the surrounding fields or forest have different values. It is an inhabited landscape where certain rocks and trees and waterfalls are the abodes of spirits. Other areas are special in other ways, associated with memories and myths. The mix of the sacred and profane, which the sociologist Emile Durkheim discussed and illustrated from the work on Australian aboriginal peoples, is clearly present.

Most people, living in the advanced urban landscapes of the west where there are few special spaces, have lost this feeling. It may be temporarily aroused by particular activities; feverish drinking on a Friday evening, a football match, a disco or wedding party. But these are only limited moments of created effervescence in a generally spiritually flat and neutral landscape.

Cambridge has always surprised me because the spaces are so demarcated and charged with different meanings. 'Holy' or 'sacred' is not quite the right word for these, although they are certainly 'set apart' in some way, as Durkheim specified. Each College courtyard, each laboratory and department, each park or bridge has its special atmosphere and feels different. It feels like a qualitatively differentiated landscape, not quite 'tribal', yet not quite 'modern' either. It is a mysterious place where memories, values, feelings seem entwined and enriched in a way which I certainly do not feel as I wander through most universities or cities elsewhere. It has an almost magical feeling of otherness, which it is impossible to pin down yet which many, I suspect, sense.

*

Closeting yourself off is a feature which is widespread in Cambridge and indeed one of its most marked features. My inner room in King's College has a series of seven doors between the outside world and myself. There are the College gates; the outer door to the staircase, the 'oak' or huge outer door which, if closed, means that no-one can disturb me; a thin baize-covered door for notices; the actual door to the outer room; a first and second door on the tiny passageway into the inner room. Instead of the number of telephones or thickness of the carpet denoting status, one's position in the academic hierarchy seems to be measured by the number of barriers a person can place between oneself and the outside world.

In that innermost sanctum, I can work in my private space, or I can invite in particular students and colleagues for the intimacy of something which vaguely reminds me of a Japanese tea ceremony. In Japan, the effect of the tea ceremony is best created by moving into timeless contemplation by crawling through a very narrow entrance, after having walked along a specially contrived 'dewy path' through rocks and mossy trees. Students arriving for a supervision in my rooms come along the semi-sacred paths beside the lawn, or perhaps even, if I accompany them, over the sacred grass itself. They move through the six doors into a place where I have no telephone, no clock and the computer, a recent intrusion, is switched off. To complete the analogy, I usually offer them a cup of green tea before we begin to work.

In this most private of inner spaces, the mind can move on silence, away from the rush and chaos of ordinary life. There is in the privacy-with-sociability a chance for real exchange and equal conversation. It is one of the thousands of quiet pools of thought distributed all over the university.

I do not call this space my 'office', which is something I have in the Department, and that has associations with administration as well as teaching. It is in some sense an extension of my private home. It is this aspect which explains the rather peculiar feel of some of the College rooms I have visited.

My own inner room resembles the description which Peter Snow gives of a typical don's room. 'Amongst the artefacts will be evidence of foreign travels—some carved black African horns or Andean figurines. There will also be small but distinguished collections of stains on chairs and carpets commemorating expensive drinks spilt over the decades. Everything looks shabby and used . . . .'[1] In my room, as an anthropologist, there are dozens of artefacts (tiny shoes for bound feet, a headhunters basket, a shaman's water clock, a Mandarin's finger-nail guard) and a wide range of green teas. And the stains of tea and inexpensive sherry circle the frayed rug from the village in the Himalayas where I did my first fieldwork.

The public and the private, and the levels of the private, the *vous, nous, tu* and the *moi* as the French put it, are carefully kept apart. This allows the mind to continue its silent toil within the extremely busy and overlapping world of Cambridge. It can lead to a kind of minor isolation, or to a sense of careful respect for other's freedom, depending on how one looks at it. The eccentricity, freedom to think crazy thoughts or behave in unusual ways which is cherished in Cambridge is one fruit of this. As I sat in King's College magnificent hall last night my Chinese visitors expressed surprise at the elaborate 'Mohican' haircut of one of the students at the next table. They said such behaviour would not be tolerated in such a place in China. I was equally surprised at their surprise at our permissive ways.

*

I have always been struck by the large amount of formal, ceremonial, behaviour in Cambridge. If we take the looser definition of 'ritual' that it is 'standardized, repetitive, communicative behaviour', then Cambridge seems unusually full of ritual. Even in other universities, and certainly in most of life, people are not seen processing around in formal costumes and meals do not start and end with graces.

When I was at the London School of Economics and School of Oriental and African Studies, I do not remember a single formal ritual of any kind. Yet in King's College small rituals are going on all the time. One possible explanation for this odd ritualization of life is historical. Unlike most universities, which were founded and

[1]Peter Snow, *Oxford Observed* (1991), 146.

developed in the period after the Protestant reformation and the industrial revolution, Oxford and Cambridge grew up in a Catholic and agrarian world. During the later middle ages there was a fuller ritualization of life. This was only partly brushed away.

Although many institutions invent some ceremonials from nothing, it is clearly easier and more convincing if one can point to many hundred years of this sort of activity. I have the feeling in Cambridge of something old and continuous in the formalized movements, costumes and processions. The effect is not ridiculous because of the buildings. Cambridge is a grand stage for public ceremonial.

*

Yet historical explanations are never complete, because we are forced to ask the question—why bother to maintain the traditions? Anthropologists have two theories to explain rituals—the expressive and the instrumental. Rituals are expressive in that they tell people about themselves and their society. They tell people that they are special, that they are changing from one status to another, and that they are all members of one group. They express these things in the way that the flocking birds of autumn wheel and cry in the sky to express their solidarity before flying off on their long journeys.

In this sense Cambridge ceremonial is clearly expressive. The traditional prayers and toasts and singing at College feasts, the little events like champagne at the end of exams, the ceremonies surrounding the May Balls, even the highly ritualized boat races, express many things. They tell both the participants and the world about the sense of belonging, of privilege, of being set apart, of movement through the life cycle, of incorporation and separation from the community. Because Cambridge feels itself special and set apart, it clings to the ceremonies and the ceremonies reinforce that set-apartness and special flavour. It reinforces elitism but also shelters and encourages those within the walls to be somewhat more adventurous.

The other approach is to see rituals as instrumental; they are tools for doing something. In many societies they move people from the land of the living to the land of the dead, or cure sickness, or ward off bad weather. From this point of view, it is more difficult to see that Cambridge rituals do much. At a banal level, the initiation of a Fellow or the conferring of a degree at the Senate House does effect that transition of status. But these are social rituals, changes in the eyes of others and not the Gods. A person can obtain their degree *in absentia*, without attending a ceremony, and no doubt, by special regulation, their Fellowship. It is a luxury, not a necessity.

This apparent absence of effective Ritual, of acts which change the world in some mysterious way, reflects a particular fact about Cambridge. Since the Reformation, with the short exception of the Marian Catholic period, Cambridge has been an Anglican institution. For many years it would not allow in dissenters and Catholics. Anglicans, as Protestants of a middling kind, set themselves steadfastly against magic, miracles and elaborate rituals. The bread and wine are commemorative—in remembrance of Christ—they are not transformed into flesh and blood. The great Chapel of King's is an expression of the feeling of holiness—but the College could in theory continue even if there was no chapel.

*

The paradox of the appearance and the reality is part of the difficulty. On the surface, Cambridge is full of sacred places. To walk through it on a Sunday or in the evening is to be flooded with the sound of bells. The sky silhouettes not only King's and St Mary's, but also Trinity, St John's and many chapels. Each chapel has had immense care lavished on it and each is very different—from the soaring sublimity of King's to the chaste 'God in a box' of Trinity and the medieval imaginings of the Pre-Raphaelites in Jesus College Chapel. With Quakers, Catholics and many others sects and creeds it is a city of religious places.

Yet many of the dons and undergraduates, while enjoying the rituals and ceremonials, do not believe that God is present. Indeed, in Colleges where the inauguration of new Fellows is not done, many senior members have not entered the Chapel for years. When I say the dining grace at King's, *Benedictus Benedicat*, let us be blessed, I take it as a social blessing. I do not expect or ask for a divine blessing. Heads of Cambridge Colleges attend numerous services and engage in many Anglican rituals, yet a number do so as agnostics or atheists and do not seem to feel uncomfortably hypocritical.

Cambridge is full of *spirit*, of a feeling of some sort of parallel field of forces, of constant formal behaviour to separate or join or stress something. It is a world of strong separations between the ordinary (profane) and the extraordinary (sacred). Yet it is not a religious community in the full sense. This double life is one which I value. There does seem to be something special and beyond the here and now about the place. Looking back over my years, the feeling that time and space should be punctuated by symbolic, formal, actions clings to me. Peter Burke comments that 'When I went to Sussex in 1962 I was relieved to be free of some of the Oxford rituals, but soon found, like the students, that the absence of rituals was more of a burden, missing especially the welcome and the farewell rituals.' In Cambridge I feel a sense of aesthetic and intellectual pleasure of being a part of something which, through its ceremonials, seems to suggest it has a kind of soul as well as a body.

Sometimes I smile at the outlandish and anachronistic rituals, at others I feel anxious that I do not understand their purposes, or how to perform them properly. Yet I am enough of an anthropologist to feel that they are probably performing an important function. They have certainly given those who live within this double world some feeling of a dimension beyond this one, though for most it is a hope that their ideas will live on.

*

Tolerance today is somewhat paradoxical, since Anglicanism was not always so encompassing. The Colleges were to a certain extent set up on an analogy with monasteries and only those prepared to enter holy orders could become Fellows. For many centuries only those who would subscribe to the established church could be undergraduates. The current King's Fellowship admission oath to maintain the place as one of 'religion' makes sense in this context.

The generally puritan tone of Cambridge, certainly from the sixteenth century and probably long before, invests the place so that it is 'lower' church than Oxford. There was no high church 'Oxford movement' here. Cambridge is Anglican, but tolerant. It is catholic with a small c, that is open to many interpretations.

This does not mean that religion was not taken seriously. Cambridge was the hub of the English reformation. Famous English protestant martyrs, including Cranmer, Latimer and Ridley, were Cambridge educated, and the compiler of the Book of Martyrs, John Foxe, was also at Cambridge. Since then, the stridency has diminished and what I have observed is a form of gently understated, private, Christianity. It is more to do with good manners, the beauty of holiness, respect for order, the acceptance that there are mysteries we have not yet fathomed, rather than a burning fundamentalist zeal. Until the Universities' Test Act of 1871, attendance at Chapel was compulsory in Cambridge Colleges. So there was, as elsewhere in England, conformist attendance, but it was not zealous: 'they go to Church on Sunday, just as regularly as they dress every day for dinner; and regard a man who neglects church, just in the same light as one who eats fish with a knife.'[2]

La Rochefoucauld noted that the multiplicity of arguments, contrary interpretations, private opinions and strong reservations, means that each person brings to their formal adherence a different vision. 'The only point on which there is general agreement is that nearly every Englishman holds a different belief; all of them believe

[2]Prince Puckler-Muskau in Wilson (ed.), *Strange Island*, 176.

in some particular point peculiar to themselves . . . . From which I conclude that the whole body, which is made up of these individual believers, believes in nothing at all.'[3]

For many, as I have discovered in my interviews, there is a sort of suspended judgement on the whole matter. There may be a God, and like Pascal's wager it may be sensible to err on the safe side and act as if there is one (which is also good for morality and social order), but the actual doctrines, dogma and beliefs are left vague.

If enthusiasm and ardent adherence is a measure of religious sensibility, then for most people there are more important 'religions' in Cambridge than what happens in the chapels. Many are more excited about other passions—rowing, rugby, drama, music, writing, experimenting, drinking, eating—than about the services they attend.

So what I see, and suspect is of long standing, is a surface of quiet conformity, a sort of slightly sentimental, slightly puzzled attention to a vague form of middle of the road, neither high nor low, extreme nor absent, set of practices. It is this which, like sacred cotton wool, fills the 'god-shaped hole' so effectively.

*

This surface of respectable Anglicanism has always been a protection. There is a considerable danger that in trying to investigate the deeper reality which lies beneath the surface of things an individual will quickly come to threaten ecclesiastical and political power. The fate of the later Islamic scientists from the thirteenth and fourteenth centuries, whose work petered out as their institutions came under religious pressures to conform to orthodoxy, to accept that all that should be known was already known, is well documented. The end of the golden age of Spanish, Portuguese and Italian thought as the Inquisition grew in power and emptied the universities of all 'heretics', burnt Giordano Bruno and threatened Galileo, is well known.

[3]Jean Marchand (ed.), A Frenchman In England, 1784 (Cambridge, 1933), 92.

The fact that even as powerful a nobleman as the Baron de Montesquieu, as late as the middle of the eighteenth century, in as enlightened a country as France, could wake up in terror at the thought that he was being pursued by the Inquisition and was forced to publish his *Spirit of the Laws* anonymously outside France in 1748, gives some measure of the normal tendency to suppression of learning.

Such suppression only happened once in England, when the flow of the Reformation was briefly reversed under Mary Tudor and the Protestant martyrs of Cambridge were burnt at Oxford. Normally it was possible to be subversive while retaining a veneer of social respectability. John Locke could not be ignored or suppressed despite his contractual theories of Kingship because he was a respectable, middle class, Oxford man. Likewise, daring thoughts questioning the whole nature of the universe and how it has evolved have continued for hundreds of years without leading to trials for heresy. Adam Sedgwick at Cambridge may have been horrified at the implications of his pupil Charles Darwin's work when he first heard about it, but he could not suppress it.

Darwin might by implication undermine the biblical account. Sir J.G. Frazer might question the basis of religion. Bertrand Russell might challenge the philosophical traditions of the west. Yet, on the surface, Cambridge was not a threat. Cambridge dons were solid, middle-class, gentlemen and 'Christians'. They went to the chapels, they said the graces, and they performed the rituals. What they thought in the inner chambers of their minds was no-one else's business. Their desire to pursue truth without fear or favour was not only their right, but also their duty. When the great Oriental scholar William Robertson Smith was accused of heresy in Scotland while at Aberdeen University, he left and came to Cambridge where he became a Fellow of Christ's College, Professor of Arabic and University Librarian.

In England now we take this separation between public conformity and private opinion largely for granted. I have shared my rooms in King's with five other Fellows. The first was a historian.

I remember him as rather devout, certainly in his attendance at chapel. In the other room was an anthropologist who I am pretty certain was an atheist, and certainly very critical of Christian missionizing, even though as Provost he had presided over many religious rituals. Later I was joined by a classicist who was proud of mentioning his partly Jewish background and was clearly fascinated by religion and wrote a good deal about it. I suspect he was probably an agnostic. For two years there was the Chaplain and now there is the Dean of Chapel next door.

What is symptomatic is that in the thirty years of sharing these rooms, meeting as friends almost every day in term time, I cannot recall a single occasion when I discussed my inner faith with any of them. None of them tried to persuade me to their way of thinking and, when I have asked their close friends about what these five believed, they admit they don't know.

One said that the historian 'worshipped the Bible but not God'. Another said that he was sure that the classicist believed something, but what it was he was not sure. I knew the anthropologist quite well through his writings, many of which touch on religion, but reveal little about his faith. The Dean has a large library of theological books but neither he, nor the Chaplain who preceded him, have ever tried to persuade me to attend chapel.

Religion is not banned as a topic of conversation at King's High Table, as it used to be (as divisive) in Oxford. Yet I have seldom discussed it, except in an abstract, distanced, academic way in relation to some particular current event or talk. So when the Chapel was visited by the Dalai Lama, or used for African drumming or Indian sitar playing, or as the venue for the first public lecture by the ex-Kingsman Salman Rushdie after the fatwa was laid on him, there seems no incongruity or dissonance.

*

Cambridge is one large sacred space, full of religious iconography, architecture, paintings, rituals and performance. It is equally true that it is a tolerant, freethinking, questioning, liberal place where people do not seek, as Queen Elizabeth famously put it, to make a window into people's souls. 'One can be a free-thinker, a Flat Earther, a Baconian, an advocate of Free Love, a Communist—any sort of intellectual non-conformist—and no one will object, provided that it does not spoil one's manners at High Table or make nonsense of one's scholarship.'[4]

This balance is creative, keeping options open, protecting against the extremes of heresy, suppression or fundamentalist intolerance on the one hand, and of vacuous chaos or extreme relativism and cynicism on the other. It gives some order, meaning and integration to life and in moments of high emotion, as in the memorial services for Fellows, it can bind the community together.

Though the Anglican settlement in Cambridge has been a broad one, for most of its history the University has not been able to tolerate everyone within its fold. Great English figures like John Stuart Mill avoided Oxford and Cambridge, or in other cases went down without a degree, because they refused to subscribe to the Church of England. Quakers and Catholics were excluded for most of their history. There has been ingrained religious intolerance alongside racial and gender intolerance.

That is yesterday's story and now people of all religions and ethnic groups are welcomed. Yet it is worth remembering this feature of most of the eight hundred years of Cambridge. Only recently has it produced distinguished black writers, artists and politicians, or encouraged peoples of religions other than Anglicanism.

Only in the last sixty years has Cambridge given full degrees to women. Calvin, of course, is more extreme than Luther in his misogynist attitude and there is a streak of anti-female prejudice in his thought. The long struggle to bring women fully into Cambridge, which has only really been won in the last half century, may owe a little bitterness to that Calvinist streak. The resistance also arose out of realization that an ancient, male, celibate, monastic institution

[4]Rose and Ziman, *Camford Observed*, 223.

would be deeply changed by the end of celibacy and maleness. The enormous impact of the acceptance of women, particularly on the College system, as well as on every aspect of Cambridge life, will be evident throughout the later account.

*

Foreigners who visited Cambridge from the sixteenth century onwards often commented on its relative austerity. This had, in fact, begun well before the Reformation—the interior of King's, for example, is largely undecorated and simple, though there is drama provided by the branching ceiling and coloured windows. The general atmosphere of Cambridge shows to a considerable extent the Protestant, middle of the road Anglicanism, that infuses it.

The virtues and vices of Puritanism are satirized by George Bernard Shaw and analysed by Max Weber in his work on the Protestant ethic. The Cambridge I have known is a living example of what Weber meant. There is the striving for salvation of some kind, the hard work, the general honesty and trustworthiness, the reserve and dislike of boasting or conspicuous display, the egalitarianism, the punctuality, the careful stewardship of resources, the assumption of the innate dignity of the other. These Protestant virtues are widespread in Cambridge. They have survived despite pressure from two directions.

The first might be termed the costs of success. It is a perennial problem, which afflicted the great medieval religious orders and affects corporate religions everywhere, that through benefactions, hard work and humility they tend to accumulate great wealth, which is then re-invested, and produces further wealth. Often the situation becomes so blatant that a powerful ruler will scythe away much of the accumulated wealth, as happened in the purges of the Buddhists in China, Japan and Tibet, or at the English Reformation.

Yet Cambridge was never completely scythed back in this way, and it is, with Oxford, conspicuously wealthier than many other Universities. This wealth is, of course, only relative. A successful author of a children's book can be as rich as one of the richest Oxford and Cambridge Colleges, and Bill Gates' fortune is equivalent to several Cambridges. The richest College in Cambridge is exceeded in wealth by dozens of individuals in the booming economies of China or India. A house-owner in many parts of Mumbai, Beijing or London is richer than many of the new Colleges.

Nevertheless, relative to other institutions of education in Britain, Cambridge has been wealthy. Its solution to the problem of being both rich and puritan is the same as that described for the Dutch Republic by Simon Schama (who knows Cambridge well as a graduate and Fellow) in his book *The Embarrassment of Riches*. In the Dutch case, while the sober blacks and whites and simple furnishings were retained, if you look closely at the cloth, the pictures, the furniture, the food and the drink, you can see that it is of the finest, combining decorum with understated luxury.[5]

It preserves a tension between Puritanism and licence which even affects some of the most important theories which govern our world. For example, it has been suggested that the economist John Maynard Keynes was influenced in his philosophy by his reaction to the various forms of Puritanism (in the arts, in sex, in College life) which he encountered in Cambridge. 'Keynes was reacting positively against the Puritan ethic: he hated Puritanism in any form and not least in the form it had long taken at Cambridge . . . . But it was his hostility to the puritan ethic which stimulated and lay behind his economic theories—spend to create work, spend one's way out of depression, stimulate growth.'[6]

*

The contradictions between restraint and hedonism are echoed in the lives of many of those who pass through Cambridge. I remember

---

[5]Peter Burke tells me that at the puritan College Emmanuel, the portrait of the founder, Walter Mildmay, shows him looking ascetic and dressed in black. When the portrait was cleaned, the black gown showed up as a luxury product, probably Genoese velvet, with an elaborate pattern.

[6]Richard Deacon, *The Cambridge Apostles* (1985), 64.

vividly the strange feeling when I first arrived in Cambridge, an impecunious student catapulted onto High Table. J.K. Galbraith described American capitalism as 'Private wealth and public squalor'. As I returned to my family in the small working class house we had just managed to buy and watched my wife clear away a simple supper, I could scarcely believe I had just come from a world of superlative wines, butler service, large warm rooms. It seemed to be public (or rather College) wealth and private semi-squalor.

This is a contrast that many visitors must feel. There seem to be parallel worlds. Inside the College context they experience something of eighteenth century country life, a reflection of the world portrayed for Oxford in *Brideshead Revisited* or *Zuleika Dobson*—gentry affluence. Yet the private lives of younger Fellows, especially if married, can often be ones of shabby gentility.

This is shown by the housing situation. It used to be estimated that one could afford a house which cost three times one's annual salary. Starting salaries for junior academics at Cambridge are approximately in the range of 20–30 thousand pounds a year— something less than a third of that of a doctor or lawyer. A research Fellow often gets only a half or two thirds of this. Nowadays a modest house in or near Cambridge costs ten times this amount. The houses where the generation above me live on the other side of the river cost something like twenty or twenty five times this annual salary.[7]

So we can see that the capitalistic monastic institutions which sustained the unmarried monkish Fellows in reasonable food, wine, furniture and comfortable rooms in the old buildings have long given way to a world where there is a huge discrepancy between College life and private life. It increases the feeling of strangeness, of parallel worlds running to different rhythms.

---

[7]As Peter Burke comments, 'a historical geography of houses for Fellows would show the shift from Adams Road to the Kite, then down to Gwydir Street, then the wrong side of the railway station, and now out to Ely as well as the villages . . .'.

SOCIETY

King's Parade and King's Chapel

King's Parade, along the front of King's College, is the centre of a city which is now known for its education, research and science parks, but also for international tourism. The Chapel dates around fifteenth to sixteenth century, the screen by Wilkins, nineteenth, and like much of Cambridge is a re-imagination of earlier styles.

[Photograph: courtesy Zhiguang Yin]

CUSTOMS

Cambridge is a customary place. It is embedded within the customs of the English. Many believe that the major justification for doing things in the way they are done is because that is the custom—that is how they have always been done 'time out of mind'. This is how it has been portrayed in the cultures which have been the traditional areas for anthropological research.

In these oral cultures, the rules of behaviour are not written down. Nor can they be specified in an abstract way by informants. Nevertheless, people intrinsically know what the customs are. They are binding, powerful and widely accepted. In such societies, as in Cambridge, the title of a well-known anthropology book is apposite: 'Custom is King'.

Anthropologists have largely abandoned the word custom, yet they have substituted other words which roughly mean the same thing such as 'habitus' from the French sociologist Pierre Bourdieu. For no-one who lives in a place like Cambridge can be unaware of the way in which most of our actions are determined through time by a set of implicit and inherited practices and assumptions. These ways of thinking and behaving, about which we are largely unaware, tend to get richer and more complex the longer a culture has existed.

They also become deeper within groups surrounded by geographical or social boundaries. England, and within England, Cambridge, is old and quite bounded and hence the customs are powerful.

A philosophical treatment of this whole issue can be found in the work of one of the twentieth century Cambridge philosophers, Michael Oakeshott. As paraphrased by Robert Grant, Oakeshott argues that 'A tradition in itself is no more than a particular way of doing or conceiving things . . . which can only be learnt by immersing oneself in them. It is a form of embodied practical knowledge which, though concrete, is not amenable to rationalisation, but which can and (since there is no alternative) must be handed on through a process of induction and apprenticeship, in the manner of a physical skill. In every practice, including even intellectual activities such as science and history, possesses this traditional character. In all, the core knowledge, however important the additional informational component . . . is of this tacit, irreducible kind, which Ryle would call "knowing how" as opposed to "knowing that".'[1] This precisely describes the situation in Cambridge where tradition, custom, 'knowing how', are incredibly important.

*

Much of the happiness and success of a student, teacher or even visitor to Cambridge depends on learning the customs of the people visited. This is not just a matter of discovering which streets are fit for bicycles, where the best pubs are, how to queue or negotiate the pavements. There are deeper linguistic codes, manners and etiquette, myths and histories to be learnt. What to talk about and what to avoid, how to give and receive gifts, what interests and persuades people, how to entertain and be entertained, all these have to be gradually absorbed.

*

[1] Richard Mason (ed.), *Cambridge Minds* (Cambridge, 1994), 229.

The Cambridge system is not too heavily based on person to person relations, on what the Chinese call *guanxi*, or is known in the literature on Mediterranean countries as patron-client relations. There are important exceptions, of course. In the History Faculty between the 1960s and 1980s, for example, there were two great patrons or academic barons (Sir Geoffrey Elton and Sir Jack Plumb), who tended to make or break the careers of a number of younger scholars within Cambridge. But for much of the time, action is based on a set of very general, unspecified, but accepted principles which have been learnt by the players, just as one learns to play tennis or football.

Surprisingly, perhaps, once a person has internalized the rules, it is efficient. He or she does not need to think about them because, like swimming or driving a car, they become part of one's personality. They become bodily and intellectual practices and it requires little extra effort to apply some very general rules to a specific case.

A second feature is that customs are durable, self-sustaining and impregnable to logic. They are like the parents' answer to all the children's 'why' questions. 'Why do we do things like this?' 'Because we've always done it like this'. 'But why have we always done it like this? 'Who knows, that is what we have always done.'

If the system is working well, there is a sense of integrated fulfilment and even harmony. Culture and Nature become elided—it feels as if this is the only sane, sensible, way to proceed. The customs of the group have become aligned with the rules of the universe. Even if occasionally one has a sense that they are out of line with much of the rest of the world, there is comfort in the thought that they are ideally fitted by long and devoted use to the present circumstances. Apparently rational arguments to change the customs, or to query their foundations, are shrugged off in some variation on 'all is for the best in the best of all possible worlds'.

A further feature of custom is that it creates a tight bond between those who have learnt the customs. A College or Department can become like an orchestra. Each person knows the customs after long use and can anticipate how others will act. It largely works on the basis of conscience and with little discussion. Only new, borderline or ambivalent cases require explicit discussion. Others who know the customs are close to one—they are of one's group. They speak the same 'language', not just words, but deeds and approaches to life. Customs bind together, in a shared being and sense of mutual responsibility, a shared history and set of conventions.

*

Cambridge is full of talk, along the paths and cloisters and even more so in the private and public spaces where a ceaseless discussion of issues from the trivial to the sublime never stops. One Nobel Prize winner, Sydney Brenner, for example described how it was through almost ceaseless conversation with Francis Crick that they worked out the implications of the discovery of DNA. At meals, after meals, in endless meetings and teachings, formally and informally, the art of conversation flourishes.

Michael Oakeshott made the 'conversational' metaphor one of the centres of his thought. He used it as 'an all-encompassing metaphor for the ideal structure of education, social life generally, politics and much else. The traditional liberal University, in which different disciplines are brought together, not in a common substantive enquiry, but in a common *spirit* of enquiry, which involves no sacrifice of any of their autonomy . . . universities, friendships, clubs, fraternities and the common life pursued within them are, like love and art, as pointless and inconclusive as conversation . . . simply ends in themselves . . . .'[2]

Peter Burke has suggested to me that there may be a link between good talk and not publishing much. He writes that 'Two of the wittiest Fellows at Emma when I arrived virtually published nothing, even a book review, but they were full of ideas about American

[2]Summarized by Robert Grant in Mason, *Cambridge Minds*, 230.

history and Russian literature respectively and were sometimes irritated to find that someone had published "their" ideas . . . . Because they had "published" orally, in College, I think they had a sense that nothing more was necessary. That assumption also links up with collegio centrism.'[3]

I have encountered the same phenomenon many times, for example when I was studying history at Oxford and a number of my most brilliant teachers were known to have only published one or two articles. Their ideas were shared within a small circle, particularly in the case of medieval historians, and were appreciated by their students and colleagues, the people who mattered. What was the point of publishing them elsewhere? But such an approach was given a bitter blow by the 'publish or perish' philosophy imported from America and endorsed by the Research Assessment Exercises.

Virginia Woolf paints a picture of one of the many such conversationalists, Sopwith of Trinity, who every evening 'went on talking. Talking, talking, talking—as if everything could be talked— the soul itself slipped through lips in thin silver disks which dissolve in young men's minds like silver, like moonlight. Oh, far away they'd remember it, and deep in dullness gaze back on it, and come to refresh themselves again . . . .[4] All this is obvious but needs stressing, for it is often thought that ideas are principally worked out by lone academics sitting silently at their desks or in libraries.

*

Yet there is also shyness. Alan Hodgkin the Nobel physiologist tells of a typical case, of a distinguished Fellow of Trinity who used to invite undergraduates to meet him every week, but would then often sit for a miserable hour in awkward silence.[5] As Hippolyte Taine earlier observed more generally of the English, 'there are men of

[3]Peter Burke, personal communication.
[4]Virginia Woolf, *Jacob's Room* (2004), 39.
[5]Alan Hodgkin, *Chance and Design* (Cambridge, 1992), 48.

Trinity College Library

The interior of Trinity College Library looking south, from Le Keux's 'Memorials of Cambridge'. The library is noted for the elegance of its architecture, the wooden carvings by Grinling Gibbons and the collection of manuscripts ranging from philosophy and science (Newton, Wittgenstein, Russell) through to children's stories (Winnie the Pooh).
[Willis and Clark. II,543]

education, even learned men, who have travelled, know several languages and yet are embarrassed in company'.[6]

It is understandable that when one is pursuing some abstruse topic it is difficult to bring oneself back to what feels like trivial

[6]Hippolyte Taine, *Notes on England* (1957), 54.

chitchat. After a few remarks about the weather or some national event, what is there to talk about? Lecturing or teaching around a focused subject is fine, but chatting about the latest development in number theory, pre-Socratic philosophy or French structuralist anthropology is not really possible. Any tendency towards introversion can be exacerbated, particularly in the early stages of a career as one pursues a very narrow topic for a Ph.D.

It is worth being aware of this streak in Cambridge. Many students and visitors have struggled to keep up a cheerful conversation with some high-powered academic they have accidentally found themselves sitting next to. They should remember that even that person's colleagues may find that conversation quickly dries up.

It may partly be the Puritan heritage of minimalism and self-control; it may be the stiff middle class education, including the often punishing effects of early separation from parents and being sent to boarding schools. It may be that certain rather in-turned personalities go with great abilities in intellectual work. Whatever the combination of reasons, it is obvious that the English *sang froid*, cold blood, the feature that can easily be mistaken for haughty arrogance, or a boring lack of emotion, is quite common in Cambridge.

An extreme example is that of the Cambridge philosopher Henry Sidgwick, as described by F.W. Maitland. Even when a close friend or colleague died, he expressed little. And Maitland himself, on the surface, appears dry and reserved, especially in his letters.[7] Yet as you probe deeper with Maitland the playfulness with his children, the love of music, the ironic humour that permeates almost every page of even his driest accounts of medieval law begins to emerge. I have found the same with many of my apparently dry and shy friends.

The reserve is also part of the delicacy and consideration that is often displayed. One aim in this virtual village is not to trample on other peoples' personal space, their ideas or their self-esteem. The approach is that of the good sheep dog, crouching patiently

[7]C.H.S. Fifoot (ed.), *The Letters of Frederic William Maitland* (Cambridge, 1965).

to let the other move and then creeping forward a little, gradually and imperceptibly guiding pupils or encouraging friends. Bullying, ordering, swaggering, rushing in like the proverbial bull is frowned upon by most, though, as we shall see, there are exceptions.

The reserve is also displayed in the well-known tendency to understatement. 'An Englishman understates, avoids the superlative, checks himself in compliments . . . .' and consequently visitors are advised 'Be modest. If you are a world tennis-champion, say, "Yes, I don't play too badly." If you have crossed the Atlantic alone in a small boat, say, "I do a little sailing".'[8]

The reserve is shown in many other ways. The normal costume of a Cambridge don, as I have known it, is usually nondescript and informal, though the patched, tweed jacket, dull tie and corduroy trousers have now given way to open shirt, crumpled jersey and jeans. The older and more tattered the gown worn on formal occasions the better, and many shoes are scuffed and unbrushed.

Even the posture, slightly stooping, moving slowly but resolutely, gazing a little into space, is often reserved and reticent. And so are the gestures.[9] As Count Pecchio asked in surprise, 'Why is it that the English gesticulate so little, and have their arms almost always glued to their sides?'[10] The English middle class traditionally did not use their bodies to gesture or to reinforce speech. It is words, not thumping fists or waving arms, that can amuse and persuade. This widespread characteristic is at its most extreme in Cambridge. I cannot recall ever seeing a colleague cry, wave his arms wildly or use other forceful body language in normal life. Games and rowing, of course, are different and all the reserve is lifted and a person is transformed into a yelling, waving, excited animal—which is presumably one of its attractions.

[8]Ralph Waldo Emerson, *English Traits* (Boston, 1884), 93; Maurois in Wilson (ed.), *Strange Island*, 260.

[9]Though, as Peter Burke comments, this is wider than Britain, being found in much of the Protestant North of Europe, for example the Dutch, Swedes and others.

[10]In Wilson (ed.), *Strange Island*, 177.

This cautious humility also makes collaborative academic life easier. In order to play in the team game in the pursuit of knowledge, each player must know his or her limits. If a Nobel Prize winner in physics thinks he can thereby pontificate on medieval history, he or she will soon be gently put down. 'The most outstanding trait of the English character' D'Eichtal suggested was that 'an Englishman never expressed opinions on subjects which he did not understand.'[11]

The rapid advances in theory and data about the world means that only by an extreme division of intellectual labour, whereby each person focuses on a small part, can understanding be advanced. To be aware of what we do not know is an essential prerequisite. When a person does speak, his or her words have added value because they have not debased the currency by asserting a certainty in fields where they only have a superficial background.

One consequence and sign of this is the relative absence of the public intellectual in Britain. In many European countries the very fact of being a senior academic may mean that politicians, the media and others will expect you to pronounce on a wide range of general issues. In England, it is noticeable that in popular opinion programmes, such as 'Any Questions?' or television current affairs programmes, hardly any academics appear.

This, of course, fluctuates. There have been periods when programmes like 'The Brains Trust' or popular books by Bertrand Russell, C.M. Joad and others showed academics being listened to, and if there is a very specific question, a regional or scientific expert may be consulted. But the way in which intellectuals are regarded in many continental countries, where high achievements in education give considerable authority, has largely been absent throughout English history and continues to this day.

*

[11]B.M. Ratcliffe and W.H. Chaloner (eds.), *A French Sociologist Looks at Britain* (Manchester, 1977), 101.

Cambridge is to a considerable extent a 'total' institution, which is what anthropologists call face-to-face, oral, multi-stranded communities like boarding schools, hospitals and prisons. One of the problems the inhabitants of such places face is the considerable danger of creating lasting offence. A Cambridge College is an extreme case in this respect.

From the middle of the nineteenth century until quite recently a person was often elected to a small College of a couple of dozen dons as a bachelor in his early twenties. This young man would henceforth eat, teach, sleep, worship and play within a tiny community. One day, perhaps up to sixty years later, he would die there and become a name on a wall. He would spend three quarters of his life with roughly the same group of people. If you fall out seriously with a Fellow then it can poison the rest of your life.

On the whole it is a highly, some would say, overly courteous place. Small gestures of opening doors, standing up when people come into the room, thanking people for small favours, greeting people warmly, all are accentuated so that people's self-worth is not damaged. Certainly amongst the older generation, there is an ethic of gentlemanly (or ladylike) good manners which is stressed. This is something which was noticed as a code of behaviour for the English upper middle class over the centuries, and it is still preserved in Cambridge—though there are always one or two brutal exceptions.

Likewise, on the whole, the most important part of a person's contribution in a University, their ideas, are treated with courtesy. Whatever one may feel about a person's talk, article, interjection or argument, it is best to cloak your feelings with courteous, if mild, enthusiasm. Of course, if this is just a hypocritical and vapid screen it is not always helpful. But the art of framing counter-arguments and criticisms in a way which does not create a permanent rift, which challenges the ideas and not the person who put them forward, is well developed.

There are several techniques for doing this which I have learnt in Cambridge. One is the device of the modulated negative. One does not directly say 'No' or 'You are wrong' when faced with something one disagrees with, but concedes a little and then expresses the negative later on. 'Yes, I see what you mean and that is an interesting approach I had not thought of, but . . . .' 'Yes . . . but . . . .' is the classic way of saying 'No' or 'I disagree' without giving offence.

In teaching, the equivalent is to start by praising one or two good points in an essay or argument. After that, most criticisms, however harsh, are accepted without too much pain. They may even do some good. A blistering attack from the start will probably be rejected as too damaging to the receiver's self esteem.

Another technique is Alexander Pope's 'damning with feint praise'. This is an important technique, especially in writing references or when asked for one's candid opinion of a colleague. If you write or say 'Actually I think he/she is pretty second rate and without much potential' it may well rebound in all sorts of ways. So you write or say of a piece of work 'It is really well written' or 'I enjoyed reading it' and say little or nothing about the argument. The trained readers or listeners will pick up the lack of enthusiasm or the absence of an endorsement for the intellectual content. It combines honesty with diplomacy in the same way as the answer of the subservient curate to the Bishop's wife, that his breakfast egg was 'good in parts' conveyed the badness without being explicitly rude.

*

The art of using words carefully to say things which are often the opposite of what you mean has perhaps encouraged the most characteristic linguistic feature of Cambridge—irony. Irony, of course, is a device which a person has to use when direct speech is inhibited in some way, by power, by social distance, by a desire to say something indirectly but effectively. It only works if there is a great deal of shared culture between the speaker and listener, so that the slight exaggeration, the mocking tone, or some other signal indicates that the remark has to be turned on its head. If one says of the Provost that he is the best thing since sliced bread, you may mean it—but the look in the eye, the sardonic tone, or the unlikeliness of the comparison may well convey one's real message.

This is a culture which has long valued wit and repartee and many jokes and witty sayings are savoured and repeated. Peter Burke told me a nice story from Emmanuel College where in the year 2000 the Fellows decided to invite partners of Fellows to the Christmas Dinner, previously only for the Fellows. A bachelor historian commented at the Governing Body: 'Master, I hope that we do not intend to do this every millennium'.

So, learning the art of irony is one of the most important skills in Cambridge. It is also important as it is sometimes used to exclude outsiders or newcomers. Many people have never been trained in this art, and indeed, from many parts of the world see it as a hypocritical, indirect and odious form of speech. It cannot be mastered without getting to know the place, the people, the history and the culture fairly well. Once mastered, it is the salt which savours many an interaction. It also binds people together in a kind of shared intimacy, as with a secret language.

Irony is milder than satire, and is compatible with courtesy, and it is courtesy which is the main theme here. For courtesy is like oil. It prevents a complex and very intricately interdependent machine from seizing up, lubricating parts which have to function alongside each other. Courtesy requires constant attention but is essential in a place where it is very easy for familiarity to breed coldness and for hidden negative feelings to become all too obvious.

A special aspect of courtesy is the way of treating strangers or new acquaintances. Cambridge is both static in that there are long-term friendships lasting decades, but it is also open and full of new friendships. Every year a third of the undergraduates and even more of the postgraduates are new. There are also many short and longer-term visitors. I am always meeting new and interesting people at seminars, committees and dinners. The difficulty is that each new meeting may conceal within it a potential for both great benefits and the reverse.

For centuries many of the Cambridge intake might look like callow young persons, sometimes obnoxious, sometimes lacking much interest in what one is trying to teach them. One day, however, they might well become great poets, statesmen, explorers, television presenters or comedians. Their memories of the place and of you may well be of value in some way. So it is prudent to treat them with respect. In fact, this applies to everyone. The rather loud-mouthed and ill-informed individual one sat next to at a dinner may turn out to be on the Committee to consider your upgrading or whether the University Press accepts your next book. In this small and inter-connected world you can never be certain. So it is sensible to be courteous and pleasant to everyone.

This courtesy is also, in the English way, a device to keep people at a reasonable distance. It is the courtesy of an old-fashioned dance, a certain stiffness and holding at arm's length, which may be relaxed later into intimacy. It is like talking about the weather, a set of rather empty, lowly charged gestures and remarks which establish a formal relationship without committing oneself too much.

*

Courtesy has to be learnt. Mistakes here can be the cause of great embarrassment. When I first came to Cambridge it was courteous to shake hands on greeting both men and women. Now one seldom does so, except to people from abroad. At that time one very seldom kissed a lady friend as a greeting, and never embraced a man. Then, through the eighties, the courtesies changed and now it is a complex art.

Which male friends does one embrace? The old rule that one did so to people from Latin (and especially South American) countries no longer holds. Is this a student one should kiss? Should one do so on meeting or saying goodbye? Inside one's rooms or publicly on the step as she leaves, on one or both cheeks, touching the cheek or not, with or without an embrace? A book could be written on just this theme of the courteous greetings and great care has to be taken in a climate of suspected sexual abuse and where many cultures meet. To kiss a Japanese visitor would be a great discourtesy, and even to kiss one's wife in front of a Japanese person is extremely rude. A short course in comparative anthropology is really needed just to become competent here.

At the heart of courtesy should be a concern for the other. All courtesy is about making an extra effort, by bodily or verbal signals, to show an appreciation for the other, to pay special attention to them as ends and not merely as means. It is very easy to become so involved in one's thoughts, happiness or misery, that one forgets the common courtesies. They become covered over by rush, self-regard, and laziness. But my grandfather's advice when I was about eight was that however shy, apprehensive or tired I felt I should enter a room or a relationship with a warm smile and a genuine awareness of the state of the other.

It is also worth noting the difficulty of disentangling oneself from the other, of saying goodbye. I remember as a first-year undergraduate at Oxford being very puzzled as to how to eject talkative friends from my rooms when I wanted to go to bed. I could hardly push them out, or even ask them to leave. I devised a method which really worked. I would invite them to stay as long as they liked, but say that I was off to my bedroom to get some sleep.

The same problem occurs in my rooms in the Department and College. Students and visitors do not always know how to leave or know when the meeting is over. If it is someone senior and sticky, I sometimes say that while I am delighted that they stay as long as they like, unfortunately I have (an invented) appointment—so we leave together and I head off round the building and return to my rooms a few minutes later. The art of gauging how time is passing without rudely looking at one's watch or clock is another skill that has to be learnt over time.

There are numerous new aspects of courtesy. Previously there was the question of how to invite people to meals, how to reciprocate invitations, how to thank people. Now this whole area is increased in complexity by the new etiquette of e-mails.

E-mailing is an area where there should be more explicit instruction since the absence of courtesy, or unfamiliarity with the etiquette, can easily hurt people's feelings—and one is unlikely ever to learn this. E-mails appear to be very informal, but I have found that a little extra energy and courtesy, 'Dear X' rather than a bare message except to close friends and in a quick exchange, combined with a rather formal ending (as in letters—With best wishes, XX) is advisable. A 'thank you' at the start and other little extra signs of attention seem to be appreciated. As for texting, 'smileys' and other new skills, I leave that to others.

The general point is that the small courtesies of everyday life within the total institution of a place like Cambridge are particularly important. It is like an elaborate game or dance where the rules and the etiquette are there for a purpose. If they are ignored it can lead to long-term embarrassment or worse.

*

Some of the people in Cambridge are celebrated for their refusal to conform. Awkwardness denotes the sort of argumentative and questioning person who abounds in many settings, but particularly perhaps in the academic world where such behaviour is encouraged by the injunction to think independently and argue strongly for one's views. The way in which such people are treated is a good index of the health of an institution.

Although the productive running of any complex organization requires a great deal of trust, commitment and judgement, it does not require that every individual within it be the same. Indeed variation is important and idiosyncrasy, individualistic deviation and contrariness is necessary to counteract complacency and conservatism and as a spur to creativity.

It is difficult to fit these people into categories because oddness is of their nature—each is different and fails to fit into normal classifications. All I can do is to give a few examples.

The archaeologist William Ridgeway sounds cussed from the accounts of the way he savagely attacked every attempt at reform at the start of the twentieth century, including those of the young Cornford. Or again, there is Oscar Browning of King's College. 'He was a genius flawed by abysmal fatuity. No one had finer gifts than he: he could think on big lines, he could strike out great ideas, he had wit, he had the power of planning largely and constructively, he had courage and a high scorn of ridicule, it was impossible to come into contact with him without being conscious of great intellectual force. But it was impossible not to be aware that he was a buffoon.' To take just one example, 'His snobbishness was of a really remarkable order . . . for, although already waddling with obesity, he took to playing hockey simply for the pleasure of being wiped over the shins by H.R.H. Prince Edward of Wales when he was an undergraduate at Trinity.'[12]

I have also met some tremendous snobs, people who look through you, drop names in every sentence, show unusual conceit about their silver or antique collections. They generally move in a haze of social arrogance which gives one a whiff of an ancient world of class competition which has largely disappeared. But again they are tolerated and even humoured, causing secret amusement as parodies of themselves, and tolerated as part of the human zoo, who suddenly do some kind and generous act to their friends or College because they have not been rejected.

Another kind of person is one who combines deep conservatism, religious fundamentalism and an attitude of constant suspicion of others. Surprisingly, perhaps, such a person can also have devoted followers who get into position of considerable power and carry their message through the higher reaches of the Church and State. At such a person's funeral, their baleful influence which has blighted a number of lives, but kept alive a reactionary and ancient streak in the University, is hinted at in the most delicate of ways.

It was observed by Konrad Lorenz that, among sticklebacks, if a certain part of the brain was removed it stopped reacting to others,

[12]E.F. Benson, *As We Were* (Penguin, 2001), 129, 131.

and became uninhibited in its actions—and often all the other carefully conforming sticklebacks followed it. There is something similar with the awkward types. The normal inhibitions caused by picking up the usually discrete signals from their colleagues, that they are being a bore, a pain, wasting time or behaving in an extreme and anti-social way, seem either to be unnoticed or deliberately ignored. Consequently they have a freedom which other, more sensitive people, consciously limit.

I knew such a person over some years. He was intelligent, ambitious, conceited and a bully. He would often pass old acquaintances without looking at them or acknowledging their presence. He would barge into meetings or conversations without embarrassment. He would come to a seminar and then get out the local newspaper and ostentatiously read it throughout the proceedings. Or he would go to sleep in the front row and snore loudly. He commented and wrote that he found most of his colleagues' work extremely boring. He made several of their lives difficult with his bitter letters. Yet to some friends he was enormously helpful and charming and his writing inspired a generation in his field. In due course he became a distinguished knight of the realm and the head of a Cambridge College. People saw the brilliance behind the rudeness and felt he was worth having around.

The contradiction in Cambridge attitudes is worth noting. Too much deviance and constant unpleasant or critical and obstructive behaviour will destroy the unity, trust, friendship and co-operation that are absolutely necessary for the working of the Colleges and the University. Yet all the time, in the teaching and research and in its general ethos, Cambridge encourages a combative, questioning, confrontational and competitive (sometimes playful) attitude. So it would be inconsistent and lead to intellectual and social stagnation to put the group first and crush the individual.

In my experience, Cambridge keeps the balance reasonably well. Personally I feel I can say what I like and behave as I want to a considerable degree. Yet if my colleagues find that I am being unfair, too extreme or just obstinate and pig-headed, I have to take account of their views and modify my rhetoric or behaviour.

In a place which encourages people to explore counter-intuitive, currently unpopular, even apparently crazy, ideas, like evolution, splitting an atom, quantum mechanics, black holes or DNA, a great deal of space must be allowed around an awkward colleague in order to allow him or her to pursue the apparently impossible. Without the salt, the meal would lose its flavour, although too much salt will spoil it. So one smiles, gets hurt, but defends these mavericks.

COLLEGES

If Cambridge and Oxford are strange this is clearly because of their unique collegiate structure.[1] As an anthropologist and historian, I have encountered many forms of associational organization, yet I still find the collegiate system puzzling. This can be seen in the difficulty I find in explaining how Colleges work to even widely travelled and knowledgeable visitors.

Like many things—happiness, love, beauty—it is true of Colleges that it is only when we try to define and describe the inner essence of something which we have often spoken about but never seriously analysed, that we realize that their meaning is elusive. The outward forms are obvious, the chapels, lawns, libraries, halls and the inhabitants are material enough. But when a perplexed new student or visitor to Cambridge asks me to explain what Colleges have been and are, I realize that I have lived within them without really understanding them.

---

[1]The central part of this chapter is based on and contains material from 'St Dominic's: An Ethnographic Note on a Cambridge College' by William Dell, published in *Actes de la Recherche en science sociales*, no. 70, November 1987. This was, in fact, written by Peter Burke and St Dominic's is his College, Emmanuel. I am extremely grateful to Professor Burke for his permission to include extracts from this article.

People have often described the Colleges as little 'tribes' and the whole of the place as tribal. There are indeed some analogies. Like certain tribes, there is very little formally instituted leadership—the Head of House has no police force or taxation system to keep his or her Fellows in place. There is often feuding both within and between Colleges. The Colleges have a corporate structure similar to many tribes. The tribal property—women, animals and other goods—is paralleled by corporate property in wine, books, buildings and lawns. Both are perpetual bodies in which the members feel part of something larger than themselves.

Yet we immediately notice some profound differences between a tribal world and what we encounter in Colleges. For example, although some tribal societies have dormitories and eating halls where they may keep their trophies, these only partly resemble the large dining halls with portraits, the Chapels, libraries and courtyards of a Cambridge College.

To find more satisfactory analogies to the College, one needs to move to a level of civilization where tribal, or at least kinship-based integration, is still strong, but the tools of civilization—advanced crafts, writing, instituted economic, political and religious systems—are present.

For the Colleges now exist within a civilization which in other ways is largely industrialized and individualistic, with few such integrated communities of living, learning and worshipping. Their continued presence feels increasingly anomalous, like a theme park or conscious drama. It might have felt ordinary enough for the first seven hundred years of its 800 year existence, but now it puzzles even the most astute observers. How can such a community continue to exist alongside a modern, capitalist, industrial, individualist and technological sophisticated civilization, and yet retain its otherness?

*

A College, in the legal sense of 'The Master and Fellows', is an economic unit. It owns and administers property which has been given to it over the ages, including farms, houses, which it has developed over time into companies, factories and nowadays science parks and shopping malls. The College itself consists of a series of buildings where the students live during term time and where Fellows teach. Additionally there are the administrative offices which are needed in order to run the College.

Students and those who come to the College for conferences pay for their rooms and their meals in hall, the students at a subsidized rate. A considerable staff of cooks, waitresses, bedmakers and others support the social side. Likewise there are numerous other staff, including porters, secretaries and gardeners.

A central role of the College is to teach students, most Colleges having several hundred undergraduates and smaller number of postgraduates. These come to study in a range of disciplines—the arts,

King's College Library at Night

Each College has its Library, many of them containing valuable manuscripts as well as books. King's has one of the oldest manor court rolls in the country and valuable collections of manuscripts including those of Isaac Newton, E.M. Forster and J.M. Keynes. Here the students can work on into the late evening after a day of lectures, supervisions, sports and clubs.
[Photograph: courtesy Borut Peterlin]

humanities, social sciences, natural and physical sciences and mathematics. The students are chosen and admitted to the College by the Senior Tutor in consultation with the Fellows in the relevant subjects. The selection is usually made on the basis of interviews, and the results obtained by the candidates in various examinations, some of which are organized by groups of Colleges.

The undergraduates are generally, but not always, taught by the Fellows of their College in the subject they are studying. The teachers are known as 'supervisors', while lectures and seminars are organized by the University not the College, as are the examinations. In the sciences laboratory work and group teaching makes Cambridge rather less distinctive.

A smaller number of Fellows, called 'tutors' are responsible for the 'welfare' of the undergraduates, on matters such as money, social relationships and careers. The system is both more personal and more individualistic and amateur than the counselling systems of most universities, though more formal counselling by professionals can be called upon if necessary.

The Chaplain is still important in the life of the College, though many students never attend religious services. In my College there is also a Dean who is in charge of the Chapel, and a Lay Dean who is in charge of various aspects of discipline.

Because most Colleges are significant economic units, small businesses and property holders, they have various officials whose prime responsibility is managing this aspect of College affairs. The chief of these is the Bursar, who oversees the income and expenditure and inspects the properties, and perhaps a Domestic Bursar to look after the buildings. Various committees of Fellows and Inspectors of Accounts advise the Bursar(s).

The teaching enterprise also needs a manager: the Senior Tutor. His or her responsibilities include the formulation of the College 'admissions policy', in other words the criteria for the recruitment of undergraduates, and also some aspects of discipline, for example the fining of students who give parties which are too noisy or go on later than permitted.

Together with the Master (or Provost), the Bursar and the Senior Tutor—with the possible addition of the Domestic Bursar—form an inner circle of power. In King's there is also a Vice-Provost, who chairs some committees and is in charge of Fellows' social arrangements and rooms. The Dean is also on the fringes of this inner circle.

The outer circle is composed of the remaining Fellows, who meet about once a month in term as the 'Governing Body'. The Governing Body is a kind of Parliament. To underline the formality of the proceedings, gowns are worn, official titles are used, and communication is channelled through the head of the College, who is in the chair.

There is an emphasis on keeping matters within the meeting. As Rose and Ziman observe of College meetings, 'It is the privacy of the business, the secrecy in which it is enclosed, that is so fascinating . . . . The Fellows gather in their gowns, the doors are shut . . . the bare decision is taken, action follows, as if the corporation were as much of one mind as an individual person . . . it is delicious to have this knowledge, to have this private world in which one is privileged to move . . . . Like family affairs, it is essentially private . . . . Nowhere is the cult of secrecy for its own sake—a cult that flourishes luxuriantly in British society—more worshipped than in Oxbridge Colleges.'[2]

The elections to various committees are also more complex and in bigger Colleges, such as King's, the Fellowship is broken into groups, sometimes by real or 'social age'—Senior, Middle, Junior— sometimes on some other principle. They also meet to discuss particularly important events such as the election of a Provost or Vice-Provost.

[2]Rose and Ziman, *Camford Observed*, 170.

The Governing Body does not make many statutes (College laws), though it occasionally modifies the statutes issued. For example, the Fellows completely revised the Statutes and Ordinances of King's College in 2007. This is a complex process involving several separate meetings and votes of the Governing Body. The main function of the Governing Body is to circulate confidential information, to debate controversial issues, and to elect to Fellowships and to membership of various College committees. The Fellows are, in effect, Trustees of a large Charitable Trust and therefore financially responsible for its running. Hence the overseeing of the accounts is another important part of the business.

There are committees for Finance, Wine, the Garden, the Library and the Chapel, to help raise money for the College, to advise on the election of Fellows. The Governing Body has the power to reject the proposals, and does this sufficiently often not to be taken for granted. On controversial issues a vote is taken by a show of hands and there are various complex rules as to what constitutes a sufficient majority.

Controversy over policies or over individuals is often acute. In King's, because it is so large and complex, it is often difficult for the centre to hold everything together and meetings have been known to be long and heated. The bonds of friendship and collegiality usually heal these differences in due course. The most likely focus of controversy is of course the election of a new head of the College. The air of secrecy is somewhat less obvious nowadays and several students now attend for what is called 'Unreserved Business' and there is also student representation on the committee which fixes the price of rooms and meals and on a number of the other College committees.

There are now not only College Students Unions but also a Cambridge University Students Union with its own magazine and website. Many students and Fellows in a College have quite a strong sense of belonging to a specific community, particularly with regard to inter-College competitions, or in periods of heightened political activism as in the late 1960s and early 1970s.

*

Solidarity is promoted by eating together. The Fellows and the students dine together (i.e., at the same tables, not simply in Hall) to mark the arrival in College of a new 'year' and its departure nine terms later. A new custom in King's is the 'Half-way Hall' feast to which students in the midst of their nine terms are invited and are joined by Fellows. In King's, at one of the special feasts at which the students are present, a Fellow is asked to give a humorous and perhaps nostalgic account of the history and culture of the College. This binds Fellows and students together for a moment of shared laughter. The choir also sings at some of the feasts, uniting the guests in another form of contemplation.

It is all too easy to romanticize the College, or at least to assume that other people romanticize it. However, it probably remains a community to a degree unparalleled by other British academic institutions. Until the 1980s, and still in the smaller Colleges, virtually everyone comes to know other members of the College by sight, while the chaplain and the head porter seem to be able to remember almost everyone's name. This was probably true in King's until the Second World War. But the numbers are now so great that it is impossible to know more than a sub-set of students, and I do not even know all the Fellows by name, although when they are elected we are introduced and enjoy a special feast together. But it should be added that the College is not a community to the same extent or in the same ways for all its members.

It is probably least of a community for the 'College servants' (the old fashioned term still used by some Fellows, though now they are usually termed 'the staff'). Relationships between Fellows and College staff are at once more formal and more personal than their equivalents in the world outside. Every summer in some Colleges, the Fellows challenge the staff to a cricket match, which the Fellows tend to lose. Elderly former students, revisiting the College, may call on their former bedmaker just as they will call on their former tutor. It would of course be easy to sentimentalize these relationships, which leave plenty of room for mutual dislike. It remains true, however, that a good Head Butler or Head Porter is as important in the life of the College, and as much appreciated by its members, as a good Master.

Yet the staff are not officially 'members' of the College. The College is formally divided into Senior Members (Fellows) and Junior Members (students), although the postgraduate students aspire to, and have in some places attained, an officially 'Middle' position between the upper and lower strata (complete with Middle Combination Room). In Cambridge the room for the Senior Members to meet is called a 'Combination Room', which I have been told is because it is here that people 'combine' before going into dinner. The Senior Members in King's are divided into various categories of a complex kind, though this has been simplified recently. There have been 'Official' and 'Unofficial', 'Ordinary', 'Life' and 'Honorary' Fellows, Fellows and Fellow Commoners, and a complex grid of different 'Title' Fellows. Each has its quota and juggling these is a complex business.

In King's there are a number of communal rooms which are important for different kinds of meetings. There are seminar and lecture rooms named after illustrious ancestors. There is the undergraduate bar and meeting place and a Graduate Common Room. There is a Fellows wine room and small octagonal sitting room where portraits of the Chapel hang and deals are supposedly done before meetings. And then, of course, each building, including a number of student hostels spread around Cambridge has its own name and culture. Because a College is an intersection between the private and the semi-public, the arrangement of space of this kind is important to the communal life.

The College is often far less of a community for the postgraduate students, who are unlikely to live in College, are often in a stable relationship with another outside the College, and are in any case oriented towards the peer-group in their field of research rather than within the College.

So far as undergraduates are concerned, the important thing is to distinguish the years, for this is a society in which age-sets are important. The first-year students, often straight from school, have plunged into a world which they find at once exciting and bewildering and obviously need a group with which to identify. Many of them do this within the College. An increasing number of students take a 'gap' year between leaving school and coming to Cambridge. Schools are also now more open and the students seem more adult than I was when I left a boarding school. Again there has been considerable change in the background of undergraduates and in the last twenty years the number of State school undergraduates has begun to exceed those from Independent schools.

First-year friendships often illustrate the influence on social behaviour of the built environment. Colleges are built round 'courts' so that access to rooms is via a staircase. Shared cooking and bathing facilities turns the ten or twenty inhabitants of a staircase into a small village, in which first-year friendships often begin. Cambridge folklore is probably correct in assuming that second-years are more outward-looking, while third-years return to the College community as the time of examinations and departure draws near.

Of course there are constant changes which affect the way the College functions. King's was one of the first Colleges to admit women undergraduates (in 1972) and I arrived more or less simultaneously. Many people remarked on how much more relaxed and civilized the College became as soon as this happened. Thirty years ago, most of the students came together in the evening for dinner in Hall with the Fellows, separated from them by a dais on which the 'High Table' stood. This dais has now gone but the table remains.

In King's many students have lunch in hall and quite large numbers have supper as well. Both are relaxed, cafeteria, affairs. They also use the College bar a good deal, where there are games machines and notices for a host of activities. This bar is, in effect, a Junior Combination Room, and it is a place where the Fellows and students can meet. In a number of other Colleges, such as Caius or Magdalene, students wear gowns and stand up when the grace is said at the High Table.

Once a term these dinners become a more special occasion, with invited guests, and once a year, in June, there is an all-night ball in College (a May Ball—though it is held in June), an expensive affair but one which quickly sells out and is often remembered with nostalgia by the participants in later years. This topic of conversation is a common one whenever 'Old Members', in other words former students of the College, exercise their right to dine at High Table twice a year with the Fellows. In contrast, King's gave up these 'May Balls' in the early seventies as elitist and over-expensive and have since had 'Events' which are cheaper and more informal.

The Fellows are the most distinctive part of the system even if this distinctiveness is not as sharp as it was. For some Fellows the College remains a community, especially if they have been there for twenty years or so or if they are one of the few unmarried Fellows and so live in College all the year round. With their favourite armchairs in the Senior Combination Room, where they drink coffee, read the newspapers, play chess and gossip with and about their colleagues. This refers especially to the 'resident' Fellows, as they are called, who give the College something of the atmosphere of an old-fashioned private hotel, or of one of the smaller London clubs.

For the married Fellows, more especially the younger married Fellows with children, the College is not so much a part of their lives, but they too are quite likely to come into dinner occasionally as well as lunch, most weekdays. However, increasingly, many scientists who work on the West Cambridge site hardly ever come into College. The convenient closeness of College and Department has been somewhat undermined with the building of new Colleges further out from the Centre and the moving of the science departments to more distant sites.

*

In this academic republic, partners are still second-class citizens, irrespective of whether the partner is a wife, husband or any 'significant other'. An exception should perhaps be made for the Master's wife, since the Master traditionally lives with his family in an official residence ('The Lodge') within the walls of the College. Until a few years ago it was impossible, or more exactly, 'not done' for Fellows to bring their wives into dinner or even lunch, although they had the right to invite guests of either sex. Inviting women into meals was an innovation, probably starting on a large scale in King's in the 1960s.

Now women have been admitted as students and Fellows, and spouses of either sex can be invited, but some Fellows are still adjusting to this change. Women Fellows may be treated with exaggerated courtesy, as if they were guests, or they may be ignored altogether. All this has changed considerably even in the last twenty years and although it is true that King's has a predominance of men and is mainly run by men, there have been women as Provost, Vice-Provost, Senior Tutor and Chaplain.

Among the Fellows, as among the undergraduates, there is a hierarchy based on seniority: not on physical age, but on what might be called 'College age'. The importance of College age is symbolized in a number of Colleges every night after dinner, when the Junior Fellow serves coffee in the Combination Room, in other words the most recently elected Fellow present. He may be a Professor or a retired General twice the age of some of his 'seniors', but junior he remains until there is another election.

It is no longer the case that the Fellows sit down to dinner, as they did in some Colleges only twenty years ago, in order of precedence according to the date of their MA degrees, but seniority has not been forgotten and is expressed in all sorts of ways. In some Colleges, the Senior Fellow presides at dinner if the Master and Vice-Master are not present, and has a special chair in the Combination Room for his use after dinner.

Socialization into the group involves becoming familiar with a body of customary law. A number of Colleges have books of customs which were learnt by newcomers. For instance in the eighteenth century at Emmanuel College anyone who took snuff in Hall was fined a bottle of claret, while anyone who was appointed chaplain to a bishop paid two bottles and anyone who bought or sold a horse paid four. It was also necessary to pay a fine for coming in with their hair in curlers or for having bought a new jacket or horse. Claret was, and still is, the currency for the settlement of bets between Fellows (entered in a special betting book), and the old law that any Fellow coming into Hall for dinner more than ten minutes late is fined a bottle is often invoked and occasionally enforced. While formal fines were and are sometimes still imposed, socialization usually takes place by means of hints, jokes, rituals and a submersion in the College atmosphere.

The rituals are the most obvious sign of the distinctive character of the community. In King's College, the 'admission' of a newly elected Fellow is an impressive *rite de passage* in some Colleges, where the ceremony takes place in chapel, with the candidate on his knees. He or she grasps the Master's hand, swears an oath to observe the statutes of the College and 'endeavour to the utmost of my power to promote the honour and interests of the College as a place of education, religion, learning and research' (an oath which does not prevent the election of atheists), after which the Master says: '*Auctoritate mihi commissa, admitto te in socium huius collegii, in nomine Patris et Filii et Spiritus Sancti*'. This is not the only occasions on which Latin is used. The ballot paper for the election of Fellows includes the words '*Ego . . . eligo . . . in socium huius collegii*' (a formula not unlike that used in papal conclaves).

Because of the grandeur of its Chapel, the inauguration in King's, with candles, surplices, oaths in Latin taken on one's knees, signing of books, introductions to all the Fellows, organ music and a feast are at the impressive end of what vaguely feels like an initiation into a special order—the Masons, Templars, Knights of the Round Table—which, of course, it is.

In some Colleges, dinner begins with a grace in Latin, using a monastic liturgical form (*Oculi omnium in te sperant Domine . . .*), and the attempt is still made to make dining in Hall into a ritualized occasion. The Fellows and the students all wear gowns. The Fellows sit on their dais like the lord and his family in a medieval hall, and the College silver is displayed on the table. The food has an obvious symbolic value, with a stress on meat with traditional high-status associations, such as venison and pheasant.

In King's on most nights there is a much shorter grace at the start and end—*Benedictus Benedicat* and then *Benedicto Benedicatur*. But at feasts and special occasions the longer grace is said. On certain evenings after dinner the Fellows move to the Combination Room to eat fruit while drinking port or claret. The port and claret are passed clockwise round the table, the port first (the rules of seniority extend in this case to inanimate objects). Here can be seen the College at its most exotic, its most archaic, the gowns, the silver candlesticks and the ritual combine to generate a certain glamour which is hard to resist. In King's there is a special Wine Room where around the walls are portraits of the famous ancestors.

There is Commemoration of Benefactors, an annual event which begins with a service in Chapel, with the recitation of the names of those who have given most generously to the College since its foundation, and also a sermon. There follows dinner in Hall and the passing round the table of a silver cup to drink the toast '*In piam memoriam fundatoris nostri et benefactorum nostrorum*'. In King's, the rituals take place first in the Chapel where there is a special service of 'Lilies and Roses', where these flowers are formally taken to the altar by representatives of the sister foundation of Eton, and of New College, Oxford, with which there is an *amicabilis concordia*.

A few days before Christmas in Emmanuel there is a domestic ritual of *communitas*, the Fellows' Christmas Dinner, with carnivalesque overtones; to wear a paper hat in the Combination Room is virtually *de rigueur*. There is also a party for the staff, which some Fellows attend. In King's the Christmas celebrations circulate focus on the Carol Services, of which there are three—Advent, the televised service broadcast by the BBC, and the Christmas Eve service broadcast on the radio. There are refreshments of various degrees of elaboration associated with these.

This cycle of observances give the insiders the comforting impression that nothing is changing. In fact there is a general awareness that everything is changing, and more specifically that the distinctive characteristics of the College are gradually being eroded under pressure from the outside world. The space of most Cambridge Colleges remains inviolate, with the public admitted only when the College allows it, but the traditional rhythm of the year has become harder to preserve, since the staff are oriented towards weekends and bank holidays rather than university vacations.

The students do not realize it was ever different, and their lives are dominated by their own three-year rhythm. As for the Fellows, their attitudes illustrate the importance of the past in the present. 'Of course twenty years is not very long in the life of the College' Peter Burke heard one of the older Fellows remarking at lunch. 'When a College has survived the Black Death' (as a colleague from an older foundation puts it), 'it learns to put other problems in perspective'. Awareness of the past, expressed in the rules of seniority and the rituals of commemoration, the visits of the older Old Members and the way in which some Fellows who died ten or twenty years ago recur in the conversations of the people who knew them, seems to go with confidence in the future.

*

Like all intense communities, there is a negative side. As Rose and Ziman observed some forty years ago, though it is less true today, 'If one is poor in a College where most of the undergraduates are well off; if one comes from a small, insignificant school; if one has fallen out with one's friends; above all, if one is shy, one can lead a solitary life, eating one's meals and taking one's walks in silence, sitting all day unvisited in one's rooms.' The economist John Vaizey writes similarly of the 1950s: 'I want to emphasize the isolation, the loneliness and the shyness which dominate the Cambridge lives of those who are not from one of the bigger schools and who lack some important inner resources.'[3] The feeling is often most acute when such a person arrives. As the poet Donald Davie writes about the same period 'I felt very vulnerable indeed—very far from home, and very much at sea among modes and codes of behaviour of which I had no experience, and to which I had no key.'[4]

This feeling is probably particularly acute, especially in the recent past, for people from other countries. 'To come to Oxbridge, to enter the courts and quadrangles, to read the names on the staircases, to dine in Hall—and then, slowly, to realize that he has not quite been accepted, that he is still an outsider; it is a poignant introduction to English life, all the more bitter, beneath the surface, because it seems so small a barrier, so mild a discrimination, that it would be unreasonable, ungentlemanly, to complain of it publicly.'[5]

Over the last twenty years, since this observation was made this feeling has been reduced. With the much wider catchment area for the College things have changed. Half the students are now women, half at least are from State schools, and many are from overseas. Talking to my students and observing their life I can see a huge change in all aspects of their life and particularly in a disappearance of much of the obvious snobbery and exclusivity.

*

An analytical account does not fully catch the sense of living among ghosts that being in an old College for a length of time can instil. So here is just a short vignette of a tiny part of that history—two

[3] In Ronald Hayman (ed.), My Cambridge (1977), 118.
[4] In Hayman, My Cambridge, 75.
[5] Rose and Ziman, Camford Observed, 109.

rooms amidst hundreds in one College, over a period of thirty years of the 550 years of its history.

When I moved into the outer room of a set of rooms (an outer reception room and two inner rooms traditionally used for a study and a bedroom) in Gibbs Building next to the Chapel (H3) in 1971 the distinguished elderly philosopher Richard Braithwaite, who worked in an inner study, took me on one side. He showed me the poker in the fireplace and explained its story. The room had for long been the meeting place for the Cambridge Philosophical Society and in the glory days there had been many long and fierce encounters between giants such as Bertrand Russell, Karl Popper and Ludwig Wittgenstein. The book *Wittgenstein's Poker* tells the story, leading up to the frustrated attempt by Popper to strike Wittgenstein with the poker, averted, Braithwaite told me, by his own timely action.

I noticed that the table I was working on had a painted surface. It was rather messy and I was wondering if it should be sanded down. I was told that it should not be touched as it was a pastiche known as 'Dejeuner sur l'herbes' by the Bloomsbury Group painter, Duncan Grant.

I constantly hear more tales. For instance, the same H3 room which I associated with philosophy was also where the brilliant mathematician John Griffiths had his room. I hear of the drinks and conversations which played an essential part in the mathematical background to the discovery of the double helix of DNA.

Later, when I became a Fellow again, I moved into the neighbouring staircase, room G2. In the other inner room was the retired Provost and anthropologist Edmund Leach. His ghost still haunts the room and I often remember the stories told of his eccentricities, some of which I witnessed. I have his slide rule, as well as the pipe once belonging to his rival, also a King's anthropologist, Meyer Fortes.

The outer room was filled with books from floor to ceiling, owned by the historian Christopher Morris. As I made my way past the groaning shelves, he would tell me of the glory days of the Political

Society (misleadingly named, being in fact the history society) which met several times a term in this room. It had been started by Oscar Browning and I imagined the ghosts of G.M. Trevelyan, Geoffrey Elton, Dom David Knowles, Steven Runciman, John Saltmarsh and many other Cambridge historians who still seem to linger there.

This outer room is now a small time capsule of the Bloomsbury period. E.M. Forster's grandfather clock stands on one wall, John Maynard Keynes' wardrobe against another, while a self-portrait by Roger Fry hangs on a third. On the fourth wall is a portrait of the seventeenth century King's College poet Edmund Waller. I have just acquired an ancient radio which belonged to the physicist Paul Dirac which is now sitting on a window seat.

I still wear Morris' gown into hall, and the tie of the distinguished classical scholar and sociologist Keith Hopkins who took over the other part of the set when Leach and Morris died. I had been lectured by him in 1967 at the London School of Economics and had never forgotten his brilliant series on Roman demography. Shrouds may have no pockets, but gowns and slide rules and ties can keep memories alive.

This feeling of being in an old tradition is part of what 'the College' is and what students and dons experience—a sense of enlargement, of being a privileged part of something bigger than themselves. The 'we-ness' is created by the usual things; the privileges of inclusion (sleeping, eating, reading, praying, playing) and of exclusion (grass, spaces, rituals), also there are the names, flags and costumes and the defining friendly team rivalries with other Colleges.

*

Even in my years in King's the people have changed greatly. Seldom does one now get quite the feeling of a fossilized older world which I glimpsed when I first arrived, but was much stronger when Virginia Woolf described what she saw in the 1930s. Here, for example, is her description of the scene outside the Chapel.

'Moreover, it was amusing enough to watch the congregation

assembling, coming in and going out again, busying themselves at the door of the chapel like bees at the mouth of a hive. Many were in cap and gown; some had tufts of fur on their shoulders; others were wheeled in bath-chairs; others, though not past middle age, seemed creased and crushed into shapes so singular that one was reminded of those giant crabs and crayfish who heave with difficulty across the sand of an aquarium.'[6]

E.F. Benson's As We Were is filled with delightful descriptions of these strange creatures in an earlier, Victorian era, and part of just one vignette of the Dean of King's J.E. Nixon, gives a sense of this strange and idiosyncratic world where 'oddness' was not just tolerated but blossomed.

'In person he was small: a short honey-coloured beard framed his chin, he had one glass eye, and only one hand: . . . He rode a tricycle intrepidly about the crowded streets of Cambridge, he played lawn tennis on fine summer afternoons in the Fellows' Gardens, taking down there a small black bag containing tennis-balls and sealing-wax and pieces of string . . . and Borneo cigars . . . . His mind whirled incessantly in a maelstrom of new dodges for counting the attendance of the undergraduates in chapel, for registering votes at Fellows' meetings, for ensuring regular supplies of toilet paper in such places as the dons needed them, or for ascertaining the speed of the train in which he was travelling . . . . On Sunday in May week at Cambridge, there was always an immense crush to get into King's Chapel for afternoon service, and in preparation for this Nixon printed a small leaflet "On the Management of Large Crowds", which he distributed to the vergers, so that they should know what to do. The crowd this year was more unwieldy than ever, and Nixon popped out of the organ-loft where he had been observing the management of it, and cried in a lamentable voice, 'If there is any more shoving, there will be no Divine Service at all.'[7]

---

[6]Jean Lindsay, A Cambridge Scrapbook (Cambridge, 1955), 7.
[7]Benson, As We Were, 127–8.

Benson describes the time when the long centuries of a prohibition on the marriage of dons was just ending. The famous homosexual friendships and love affairs in King's, Oscar Browning, John Maynard Keynes, E.M. Forster and later Alan Turing and others, is a part of all of this scene which has also largely disappeared or been accepted as part of the main stream of British society. For a while the illegal and publicly stigmatized affairs were sheltered, like other forms of deviance, within the ancient walls.

Although there was no such figure as Nixon when I came to King's in 1971, I have met a number of eccentrics. There was one who slept under his dining table, another spent some afternoons stretched out on his sitting room floor gazing at the ceiling, another kept a boa constrictor in his office which he fed with white mice from the laboratories, another built a bathroom half-way up his College set and gave supervisions from the bath. Another answered telephone calls in a succession of animal cries, others wandered around talking to themselves, one ran down his lecture-room stairs with a board pointer nearly impaling students, another shot arrows across his classes. A particularly distinguished one went to sleep and snored at the feet of nervous lecturers, another received the food for his dog through the window in the middle of supervisions, and several had rooms so filled with mounds of paper that it was impossible to reach them.

The eccentricity was accepted and even prized. Thus many fond stories are told of eccentric ancestors. Just one example describes the great mathematician G.H. Hardy, now particularly remembered for his collaboration with the Indian mathematician Srinivasa Ramanujan. Hardy would not wear a watch or use a fountain pen or use a telephone if at all possible. His New Year resolutions on one occasion were, Robin Wilson reports,[8]

---

[8]Peter Harman and Simon Mitton (eds.), *Cambridge Scientific Minds* (Cambridge, 2002), 215.

1) prove the Riemann hypothesis
2) make 211 not out in the fourth innings of the last test match at the Oval
3) find an argument for the non-existence of God which shall convince the general public
4) be the first man at the top of Mt Everest
5) be proclaimed the first president of the USSR of Great Britain and Germany
6) murder Mussolini.

The Colleges are neither modern, flat, single-stranded and functional entities, nor simply traditional and ancient units, largely based on kinship and an oral culture. They are to some extent an answer to the search for alternatives to the rootlessness of modern life and to Max Weber's 'iron cage' of over-rationality and the disenchantment of the world. They are like flies in amber, embalmed pieces of medieval life which co-exist with the modern world. This gives them the feeling of magic, strangeness, which many feel but cannot quite put their finger on.

The strangeness and the secret life evaporates under too much scrutiny, but we notice it in the corner of our eyes when we are looking at something else, for instance at scientific creativity, or friendship, or the process of growing up. Its purest expression is in the stone and glass and music of King's, but it is distributed less in the architecture than in the curious nature of social relations. These are best understood through comparing this semi-community with other groupings in Cambridge, and examining the customs and ethos of the world within which the Colleges exist.

COMMUNITY

One of the reasons why Cambridge seems rather strange and 'out of time' is that it has for long been to a certain extent a 'total institution'. With many dons now married, and many working well away from the Colleges, this has changed greatly in the last half century. But still for undergraduates in term-time and nowadays for a few resident Fellows, we see a glimpse of this rather unusual situation.

In our modern individualistic and highly mobile societies there are few such encompassing worlds. Those that do exist are usually there because people have, somewhat involuntarily, been placed in them; boarding schools where children are 'sent', hospitals, mental institutions and prisons. Another two main forms likewise cut off from the community, but based on choice, are monastic institutions and the army. Cambridge is very much a part of society and absorbs ordinary people for short periods and it is voluntarily entered. Yet there is also a certain totality about the place.

The central feature of all these total institutions is that different parts of life occur within one physical space—sleeping, eating, drinking, sport, prayer and thought. The walls, literal or virtual, are there to form a strong boundary between 'the outside' and the intensely overlapping worlds within.

When Cambridge Colleges were first built they were like monasteries. The Fellows were there for life, could not marry, slept, ate, prayed, played and thought in one physical space. A College nowadays always has the facilities for eating and drinking, the social centres of bars and the often splendid dining halls, most have Chapels for worship, libraries and studies for thought, the grounds for play.

When I try to explain to a visiting scholar from Nepal or China how Cambridge works I ask them to imagine the quadrangle of my College as a Newar courtyard in Nepal, or a clan village with its ancestor hall in parts of traditional China. There is one marked difference, however, and this is the root of the puzzle. The Nepalese

King's College Dining Hall

Eating together, as here in King's College dining hall, is a central expression and encouragement to community, as it has been from the medieval foundations of the Colleges. This nineteenth century re-creation of a medieval hall reminded a visitor of a Chinese ancestor hall.
[Photograph: courtesy Borut Peterlin]

and Chinese examples are based on kinship, while Cambridge attempted to set itself against kinship as a basis of recruitment. Fellows were not allowed to marry and so could not pass on their position to their children, although they might sometimes do so to their nephews.

It is this mixture of total institution, but one which is not based on birth or even a perpetual vow of membership (monastic) but rather on choice and supposed merit, that makes Cambridge feel such an odd hybrid, a 'total' institution based on competitive, achieved, admission. It is to a considerable extent a 'community' in sentiment and identity, based on the unities of place and a feeling of shared identity, but not on blood. It thus has two out of the three criteria for true community specified by Tönnies and others. So how does it work?

*

One way to think about Cambridge is to use the ideas developed by one of its most famous lawyers (and Master of Trinity Hall), Sir Henry Maine. Drawing on Roman Law and his experience of Cambridge, Maine elaborated the idea of the corporation, that is a constructed set of rights in property and people *which never dies.*

A western corporation is set up by a conscious act—a grant from the State giving it delegated powers. It is endowed with many of the attributes of a fictive person. It can hold property in common, it has limited liability and it joins or incorporates people. It can last forever. Individual members hold things in common or in some kind of shared way. Each member is like a limb, a head, feet, arms, of a body (*corpus*)—joined to each other and drawing sustenance from each other. To lop off the Master, the Bursar, the Dean, is like cutting off the head, arms or heart of a College.

Maine's fruitful idea was found to be applicable not only to Cambridge but around the world as anthropologists tried to understand the various ethnic groups being incorporated into the British Empire. Kinship groups, or descent groups as they are known, operate in much the same way as Cambridge Colleges. They hold tangible and intangible property in common and are perpetual. They bind the members not through blood alone, but through marriage and the selection of a principle of descent, through males or females. With the concept of corporation, anthropologists found a solution to the problem of what maintained social order in societies without a centralized state.

Reversing the idea, we can see the Colleges as equivalent to descent groups, that is clans of people who have a corporate unity and identity. But while anthropologists recognize that many of the bonds in a descent group are fictional, or constructed, this is carried to a much further extent in Cambridge Colleges where people are almost entirely recruited on non-kin lines.

The existence of a perpetual, property owning, corporation or College, among other things, gives the members of the group a feeling that they belong to something larger than themselves. In monasteries and nunneries this is expressed and reinforced by the use of quasi-kin terms, for the members call each other 'brother', 'sister', 'father' or 'mother'. For various reasons this does not happen in Cambridge. Although one of my senior colleagues addresses all of us in his emails as 'Dear Chums', this is also not exactly the word, with its evocation of Edwardian adventure stories. The chosen word is 'Fellow'.

*

'Fellowship' denotes equality, friendship, closeness, but also (implicitly) a separate identity and dignity. There are many varieties of Fellowship—Senior and Junior, Life and Honorary, Official and Unofficial, but they are all Fellows and should treat each other not merely with respect but as instituted friends.

Fellowship generates sentiment, a feeling of closeness and being of one body, but, just like a family, it does not necessarily generate affection. You don't necessarily like all the Fellows, just as you may not like some of your family. For many purposes, whatever your personal feelings, you feel some sense of respect, closeness and trust.

When I recognize Fellows on the streets of Cambridge, I greet them.[1] When I sit down next to one of them at a meal, I feel a sense of shared identity. This takes away a little of the isolation and separateness which is a strong feature of the individualistic English.

The secret, I suppose is the feeling of a shared purpose. You are a team, but not one that is trying to score the most goals, or win a race, but together you are trying to push forward the task you accepted in the oath you took when you joined the Fellowship. Jointly, you are trying to promote the College as a centre of 'education, religion, knowledge and research'.

It is this sense of shared task, ineffable yet rewarding, which sometimes spreads to others in longer-term contact with the College—porters, secretaries, gardeners—which helps to explain an anomaly. This is that while the written contractual obligations of a University teacher or Fellow are often almost non-existent, I have found myself doing many extra hours and tasks beyond the limit of the call of duty derived from some diffused sense of obligation, debt, desire for approbation, or desire to reciprocate the perceived efforts of others.

Of course there are a few 'free riders' and minimal participants, and there are times when I put in more effort than at other times. Yet it is generally the case that a sense of privileged belonging, a desire to be thought of as worthy of the Fellowship or the University, is a nebulous force which drives me on. The University and College become something like the Protestant idea of God—constantly there, watching, praising, encouraging and occasionally showing signs of disapproval at some failure or lack of effort.

*

The Charity Commission is in charge of a multitude of different Trusts, from the very large, like the Catholic Church in England

---

[1]Though Peter Burke tells me that in Emmanuel in 1980, one did not greet Fellows.

and Wales, to the medium-sized ones like the Cambridge Colleges. These Trusts are part of a system which is a complement to the idea of corporations. For there is a great danger in corporation theory in its Roman form and as applied undiluted in Roman law countries. Henry Maine's successor, the Downing Professor of Law at Cambridge, F.W. Maitland, pointed this out. Maitland's theories take us to the heart of the mystery of Cambridge.

Corporation theory is not sufficient to explain the distinctive success of Cambridge. Corporations existed all over Western Europe. Yet in France, Germany, Italy and elsewhere they did not lead to a continued, flourishing, set of independent universities after their early successful beginnings. This is because, as Maitland shows, corporations are in essence created by rulers. Their independent life is given to them as a conditional and withdrawable gift by royal power.

Maitland uses the metaphor of breathing life into dead matter; the corporation comes to life through the kiss of a charter from the ruling power. And at any time the State, if it feels the corporation is too powerful, too independent, or refuses to pay enough taxes, can turn off the oxygen. Some supplementary legal model or device is needed to explain what happened in England.

A further problem with corporations is that they do not create the warmth, the sentiment, which is needed to make people work closely and well together. To be a member of a big corporation does not necessarily mean that one feels any special affection or diffused obligation to do more than the bare minimum.

So what created the affect, and overcame the dependence on the State?

The answer which Maitland gives is the Trust. The Trust was originally a legal device used in the Middle Ages by the rich in order to avoid death duties. A fictive person, a body of trustees, was set up. They held some rights in property 'in trust' for the use of a person's heirs after they died. Quite soon the model spread out to provide the template for institutions as varied as the Inns of Court, the Stock Exchange, Lloyds Insurance, the Methodists, the Public

Schools, the Trades Unions and the London Clubs. Although the University is somewhere on the borderline between corporations and trusts, the Colleges, by outright gifts of property from royal and other donors, are in effect independent.

With the model of Trusts all around them, the University and Colleges were treated and acted as if they were Trusts. They were, in modern terms, quasi-autonomous non-governmental institutions. The Master and Fellows were entrusted with the maintenance and good governance of the College. The Colleges are in effect Trusts in the terms of the Charity Commissioners and we are often told as Fellows that we are officially Trustees of the College.

One of the most difficult and scarce commodities in all spheres of life is trust, that is the ability to take the risk to share and exchange whatever is the scarce resource—love, wealth, reputation, power—with others. Where trust exists it greatly increases efficiency and effectiveness since people can work together without the friction of checking and testing, without the inhibitions of competition and secrecy. Trust is usually in short supply; its presence is the exception that needs to be explained. As Maitland shows, this not only gives the Colleges and University a legal framework for perpetual liberty and independence, but also induces trust and loyalty.

*

One of the greatest pleasures in my time in Cambridge is that I have usually been able to trust my colleagues, both in the Department and the College. On the whole, the presumption has always been that ideas, opinions, reputations are safe with my friends and colleagues. If I ask their opinion, I assume that they will try to be helpful and truthful. I assume that they will try to put the general good of the organization before their private desires and ambitions as much as possible. This trust also extends to my students, who have almost universally shown themselves worthy of this trust.

In academic life this is not just important in running the organization, in writing and reading references, evaluations or feedback about ideas and people. Also at a deeper level it is absolutely essential for the co-operative pursuit of knowledge in any field. The warmth which being charitable and trusting towards others creates is one of the joys of working in Cambridge and it is, I believe, one of the very most important clues to Cambridge's intellectual eminence and the attraction it exercises over those who come here.

However, Cambridge is not an oasis of trust in a desert of distrust. Emerson in the middle of the nineteenth century wondered 'Is it the smallness of the country, or is it the pride and affection of race,—they have solidarity, or responsibleness, and trust in each other.' And he noted that 'Private men keep their promises, never so trivial.'[2] Around the same time, Samuel Laing, comparing continental Europe to England, wrote that 'In all the common business of trade, even to the greatest amount, mutual reliance, not mutual distrust, is the rule; and transactions in the ordinary affairs of life depend upon the good faith, the word, the custom of the parties, much more than upon legal deeds and written contracts of fulfilment.' He also wrote that 'Confidence, moral confidence, between man and man is the peculiar characteristic of the spirit of society in England. It is the lay religion of the English people . . . .' adding that 'This mutual confidence in, and dependence on, each other for what is right, fair, and reasonable between man and man, creates what it relies upon . . . .'[3]

It is this characteristic of trust creating trust that I have normally encountered in Cambridge. However, there is a danger that it is being undermined by accountancy culture and bureaucratic suspicion, by the often undermining and time-wasting efforts to justify and promote oneself in the periodic Research Assessment Exercises and other uncomprehending reviews. Yet it still survives in an unusually effective way.

*

[2]Emerson, *English Traits*, 79, 91.

[3]Samuel Laing, *Observations on the social and political state of the European people in 1848 and 1849* (1850), 290.

The Trust was the original model for the English club. In defining what is special about Cambridge it is worth thinking about how far Cambridge is a club.

The central feature of a club lies in its organization. It consists of a name—the Athenaeum or the Lode Social Club. It has some premises, permanent or hired. It usually has some other assets—a library, a games field, or whatever is necessary for pursuing its special aims. It has a management committee and some officers—President, Treasurer, and Secretary. It sometimes has a flag, motto, or symbol of identity, a tie, a shirt or other marker. If it is highly prestigious like the Royal Society or British Academy, it spends a lot of time discussing who may be invited or allowed to join it.

In all of these respects both the Colleges and the University of Cambridge seem to be large intellectual clubs to which one belongs. They overlap with London clubs, the Inns of Court and many others. The atmosphere of the Senior Combination Room feels very much like that which I have observed in London clubs. So the Colleges are indeed clubs. It is legally possible for University Teaching Officers in Cambridge not to belong to a College. If they do not join a College, either as a full Fellow or in some other association such as Director of Studies, their obligations are minimal and they can get on with their research and keep their administrative duties and undergraduate teaching to a reasonable level. But in a city of clubs, most people feel excluded if they have no College attachment and many enjoy the conviviality and sense of belonging, even if it also entails extra work and duties.

*

Cambridge may have that powerful feeling that once a member of the University, Department, College or whatever, you have a certain automatic bond with other club members. Yet there is one big difference which makes it much more than a club.

The central feature of a club is that it has one overriding and usually quite specific goal. It is set up to join people together who want to play chess, football, cricket, row, sing, run, fly, debate or engage in any other activity. Even the big London clubs, while bringing together people from many walks of life, have a particular aim—conversation, meetings and entertainment for example.

It is true that the general goal of the College is also a defined one—'education'—but education is a very broad category. Obviously Colleges have been principally set up to teach, but also to encourage research. The oath also specifies the upholding of 'religion', though nowadays this is largely left in abeyance. And furthermore, the methods of learning extend far beyond formal instruction. An undergraduate or graduate coming to Cambridge is not just learning the contents of a subject, but a way of thinking and, so it is believed, a way of life. The University is meant to instil a set of values, a morality, a mentality, a set of manners, etiquette, a philosophy, a set of bodily practices, and an invisible attitude to life or *habitus*.

The College is not merely a body, it is an ancient and living body, a 'We' that has existed for centuries and will, hopefully go on for ever. Again as Rose and Ziman put it succinctly, 'Religion itself has largely fled from the Colleges—but the cult of the College remains. It is far more than buildings and quadrangles, far more than boats and tennis courts, than dinners and tutorials. The College exists in history; it exists in all its members, resident and non-resident. A don of high historical sensibility may remark that "*We*" once owned a certain estate—and cannot tell whether he is talking of the sixteenth century, the nineteenth century, or of his own life time.'[4]

In some ways, the Colleges can become the object of a secular cult. 'The best of their values are independent of time and context . . . . The experience is mystical; it attunes one to the poetry of existence . . . . Poetry is magic; it is not surprising that a College still stands at the centre of a secular cult. *Its* existence is more than us. *It* has

[4]Rose and Ziman, *Camford Observed*, 245–6. Peter Burke comments, 'I have caught myself telling visitors that "we asked Christopher Wren not to destroy the Long Gallery when he was building the Chapel"!

claims upon us beyond rational necessities . . . the old men . . . are the Elders amongst the priests of the shrine, and we cannot help being moved by them, for it was they who initiated us into its mysteries.'[5]

*

All this talk of trust and warmth tends to paint a largely positive picture of Cambridge. Indeed my experience has been, on the whole, positive. But my own diaries remind me that there have been periods of loneliness, of frustration, of exhaustion and of deep anxiety. Cambridge can be stressful and even isolating and there have been times when I have felt a great desire to leave it, or at least take a rest. One safety valve has been the instituted sabbatical leave which in Cambridge means that every seventh term one can take a term away on full pay.

Undergraduates are often desperately unhappy for a variety of reasons and postgraduates are often lonely, for research can overwhelm a person with its narrowness, boredom and anxiety about not achieving enough or with financial worries. Foreign research students often suffer the most, since they also have to deal with homesickness, the strangeness of British culture, the weather, and the food. Married research students, with the added problems of the possible unhappiness of their spouses and conflicting pressures of family life, are in the worst of positions.

Even the dons, despite their idyllic surroundings and companionship are often unhappy, the work increasingly unsatisfying. 'He may know, well enough, that he must expand his thesis into a book— but by the fourth, fifth or sixth year it has gone a bit dry and stale on him, and he would prefer to do something else. He knows that it was too narrowly conceived, that he is narrow, that the academic groove is narrow' but he must stay in it now.[6] The decline of productivity in later life is amusingly noted by D'Arcy Wentworth

[5]Rose and Ziman, *Camford Observed*, 247.
[6]ibid., 119.

Thompson who described the fellows of a mythical Cambridge College as mostly 'of the cobra kind. They had swallowed their intellectual goat in early life, and were passing through the years of inactivity requisite for digestion.'[7] The pain of indigestion is added to nowadays by the anxiety caused by the pressure to produce a stream of important works at short intervals in order to satisfy the various research assessment exercises upon which funding depends.

A picture which leaves the reader with the idea of a placid College and Departmental life would be very distorting. The stronger the bonds of community, the more bitter the feuds and factionalism. I have witnessed a number of savage altercations and found myself filled with rage and disbelief. These disputes are often about power, privilege or reputation, but will focus on the seemingly trivial subject of the layout of the Fellows' Garden, or the purchase of a piece of furniture.

It is probable that the intensity of these feuds have lessened as the students and Fellowship have begun to come from a wider background. Peter Burke comments that 'At Emmanuel, the postgraduates were often foreign by 1980, but the Fellowship was like the undergraduates, entirely Anglophone—we had a couple of Australians and a New Zealander. Between 1980 and now we have elected, first as Research Fellows and then as Official Fellows, and not counting black British or British Sikhs, citizens of France, Germany, Italy, Serbia, Romania, Iran, Taiwan, while the undergraduates have remained 90% British.' I have witnessed the same change in King's, and with the oxygen of people from all over the world, the feuding, but also some of the warmth in a shared culture, has evaporated.

On the whole, the recipe seems to work. Yet, somewhat paradoxically, the more it works and Cambridge is enjoyed and admired, the greater may be the final bitterness at having to leave it. As Rose and Ziman write, 'Many graduates leave Oxbridge

[7]Quoted in Garrett, *Cambridge*, 89.

labouring under a burdensome sense of loss, disillusion and defeat. They suppose that there is a deep cleavage between the values of Oxbridge and the values of the world outside. For these values— the cult of personal relations, the aesthetic enjoyment of life, freedom from authority, dislike of hierarchy, contempt for material considerations, the admiration of pure intellectual skill, the disinterested pursuit of truth, a spacious, speculative and untrammelled approach to life—they have often developed a passionate liking and respect. Their mere acceptance of these values makes it painful—almost humiliating—for them to recognise that they will have to earn a living at some plebeian but useful task . . . . The prime basis for their diffidence is that they feel that they have been educated for a social structure that no longer exists.'[8] More mildly, as one final year undergraduate put it to me, 'It seems very rude when they ask us to leave'.

Yet, to end on a more positive note, for many others, after a feeling of rejection, or at least sadness, there is a heightened sense of the feeling one gets after a wonderful holiday or honeymoon. It was fun while it lasted, a never to be forgotten experience, but now one must get on with life.

*

I have spent much of my life as a historical anthropologist refuting the myth that the small nuclear family has only recently emerged from larger kinship groupings in England, supposedly as a result of the industrial revolution. I think that the present small family system goes back as far as the records exist.

Cambridge is a good example of this unusual anti-familistic tendency. It was recognized from the start that perpetual, wealthy, foundations would have a tendency to become a family business. Warmth and obligations towards offspring and nephews would have to be kept at bay if this was to be avoided. The obvious solution was

---

[8]Rose and Ziman, *Camford Observed*, 237.

not to allow people to have sons and daughters and, if possible, to limit the number and hold of nephews. So for over three quarters of its existence, Cambridge Fellows lost their Fellowships if they married. A College was like a monastery. The elaborate arrangements of servants, kitchens and rooms provided an alternative to the support of kin, assuring lodging, food, drink and help until death.

Yet in practice, kinship has always played some part in Cambridge. The Isaac Newton family never came to colonize the place, but to a certain extent other families have done so. This does not seem to be a straight matter of favouritism, but rather of a loose network of inter-relations of cousins and second cousins. Noel Annan has investigated the actual kinship of these families[9] and it is apparent in a number of the interviews I have made of leading scientists (Keynes, Huxley, Bateson, Hill). Among these families were many of the great Cambridge names and many of outstanding merit. They also intermarried with the Bernals, Waddingtons, Braggs and others who formed their own kinship linkages across the university.

While these families never became formal groups, and I know of no evidence that family favouritism rather than ability was the reason for their success, there is obviously an interesting counter motif or shadow of kinship here. The golden age of Cambridge in the later nineteenth and early twentieth centuries is suffused with stories of large houses and parties and performances in which these 'cousins' would meet and form loose, useful, contacts. One member of the Darwin-Wedgwood dynasty, Gwen Raverat, in her *Period Piece*, lovingly portrays some of this world.

Peter Levy provides a description of such inter-related cousinhoods. 'The Darwin-Wedgwood-Cornford-Raverat clan frequently held very large gatherings of the extended family; and the presence of Maitlands, Huxleys, Fishers, Keyneses, Vaughan Williamses, Trevelyans, and Peases reminded them that they were part of a world that also included Tennysons, Macaulays, Hodgkins, Arnolds, Penroses, Wards,

---

[9]See Annan, *The Dons*, Annexe.

Frys, Booths, Potters, Stracheys, and Stephens. They knew that this world was privileged, but were proud that it was also civilized.'[10]

As Levy points out, this was partly caused and re-enforced in this period by the fact that Cambridge in particular recruited Quaker families—Gurneys, Barclays, Cadburys, Rowntrees, Frys, Gaskells, Sturges, Hodgkins, Foxes and Hoares, who were intermarried. It was also encouraged by the arrival of a number of philosophical radical and Unitarian families 'whose chief representatives were the Wedgwoods, Darwins, Trevelyans, Martineaus, Huxleys and Stracheys.' He suggests that 'They preferred Cambridge to Oxford, possibly because the Tractarian Movement frightened evangelical families, and certainly because Cambridge, ever since the Civil War, had the more pleasant associations for nonconformist families.'[11]

This particular phenomenon, the rise of a certain part of the Victorian middle class, is one of the secrets of Cambridge success throughout the last century. 'An environment where creative behaviour is encouraged and expected is a great stimulus to creative behaviour, for it is conducive to intellectual boldness and a spirit of adventure. A tradition of such behaviour explains in part why the group produced such an enormous quantity of men and women of distinction.'[12]

The effects on this loose group are well described by Levy. 'Great things were *expected* of such a child. Being a member by right of birth conferred a sense of security crucial to the accomplishment of great intellectual deeds . . . . It is important to note that this intellectual elite is properly regarded as an aristocracy, for one was (and some still are) born into it . . . . It was an open-ended group, in that meritocrats could marry into it . . . .'[13]

[10]Paul Levy, G.E. *Moore and the Cambridge Apostles* (1979), 21, where there is also a kinship diagram of the connections.

[11]ibid., 27.

[12]ibid., 26.

[13]ibid., 26.

This largely informal and rather invisible network, like the other societies and clubs and associations which are so important in academic life, is another factor which helps to give Cambridge a particularly entangled feeling. It is not a large clan, but some people are related. Reading the *Annual Reports* of Colleges, it is interesting how often there is an approving remark that so and so was the son or grandson or nephew of another earlier undergraduate at the College. Parents are often keen to send their children to 'their old College'.

*

English snobbery has a particular flavour. It is based on a central contradiction. As many have noted, English class has never developed into a 'caste' system, that is into a fixed and rigid hierarchy based on impermeable, blood-based, strata. As Tocqueville remarked in the nineteenth century, 'England was the only country in which the system of caste had not been changed but effectively destroyed.'[14] Wealth and a change of accent, as satirized in Bernard Shaw's *Pygmalion*, can move a person up the social system. There has never been a proper blood nobility or a blood-based gentry. In this sense, England has always had an 'open' social system. 'English history is aristocracy with the doors open. Who has courage and faculty, let him come in. Of course, the terms of admission to this club are hard and high.'[15]

Combined with this, and indeed no doubt partly caused by it, is an obsession with class and status. 'England is the most class-ridden country under the sun. It is a land of snobbery and privilege . . . .' as George Orwell observed.[16] There is an infinite set of minutely graded differences, with an ever present chance of rising into a higher one,

[14]Alexis de Tocqueville, *L'Ancien Regime* (1856), tr. M.W. Patterson, (Oxford, 1965), 89.

[15]Emerson, *Traits*, 134.

[16]Orwell, *Lion*, 52.

or slipping downwards. So class rivalries and snobberies have been a central obsession with the British. We only have to think of the work of Thackeray, Austen, Trollope, Mrs Gaskell, G.B. Shaw, Oscar Wilde and Nancy Mitford to bring this to mind. As Stendhal wrote about England, 'Society being divided as by the rings of a bamboo, everyone busies himself with trying to climb into the class above his own and the whole effort of that class is put into preventing him from climbing.'[17]

Cambridge can therefore be seen as a powerful machine for establishing class. The University manufactures 'distinction'. Yet the social background of those who have come to Cambridge has varied. We tend to look back to the eighteenth and first half of the nineteenth century and think of it as traditionally taking members of the aristocracy, the gentry and the upper yeomanry. But for its first four hundred years it had a much wider social recruitment. For example Elisabeth Leedham-Green comments that from the thirteenth to fifteenth centuries 'The great majority of students were probably of yeoman stock or their urban equivalent.'[18] This is what one might call the middle middle-class in modern terms.

It was particularly between the eighteenth and mid-nineteenth century that Cambridge trained people in 'manners', giving them the connections and self-confidence, and gracing them with the social cachet of having been to Cambridge. For the rest of their lives they could regard themselves, and were usually regarded, as part of that prosperous, educated, liberal upper middle-class. They were the professional people, the gentry and the rulers.

Writing of the Victorian and Edwardian periods, Rose and Ziman note that 'The Public Schools and the reformed Universities constituted a single educational sequence for the sons of gentlemen

[17]Quoted in Wilson (ed.), *Strange Island*, 164.

[18]Leedham-Green, *Cambridge*, 25; she notes that Roger Ascham in the sixteenth in *The scholemaster*, lamented the general disinterest of the nobility and the landed gentry in such a form of education.

and of others who could pay for it. From the Lower School at Rugby to Degree Day at Oxford, boys were being prepared to take their place as officers in the chain of command of a stratified society.' It had a great effect everywhere. 'It is the sun round which a great many other institutions of Lower and Higher Learning see themselves as revolving.'[19]

The bewigged figures who gaze down at us from the portraits in the dining halls or are remembered on plaques and stones were largely confirmed in their position by the process of passing through Cambridge. Others were the sons of rich merchants or farmers of a more lowly background who had used Cambridge as part of their strategy to move up into a higher rank.

Nowadays, of course, it is more complicated, and the situation is perhaps returning to that which prevailed earlier in the history of the University, where it takes people from a more varied background. Though Cambridge is still a natural step for clever children from the Independent Schools, it is also increasingly attracting children from less privileged backgrounds. Furthermore, there are many foreign students of indeterminate standing, obviously modestly wealthy but with hazy social credentials.

There is not, and never has been, a carefully thought-out strategy or programme to indoctrinate people in class-consciousness or the tools of social elevation. It is just assumed that spending three years in an upper middle-class environment will shape people. Accents will be smoothed, manners, etiquette and linguistic tricks learned, they will gain the tastes in food, pictures, furniture and general culture, so that they can live a comfortable middle-class life after University.

All this is an informal matter. I do not remember ever discussing what was happening when I was a student or in my years as a don at Cambridge. Alison Richard comments that at Yale, where she was Provost, she had noted that somehow, without formal training, young people, who had come up with no ability to shake hands and held

---

[19]Rose and Ziman, *Camford Observed*, 231–2.

out limp and awkward hands in the 'hand-shaking' ceremony at the start of their course, by three years later had mysteriously learnt the art of the positive and clean hand-shake.

The subtle pressures to adapt to a set of implicit codes can cause bitterness or confusion in some. It is especially puzzling for foreign students, who may not realize that they are entering a world where gestures, postures and words carry a particular significance to some of the local inhabitants.

Of course, social position is now pretty confused and contested. In my own Department, for example, the majority of the teachers are no longer middle-class English men. Most come from other parts of the world, half of them are women, and they do not snugly fit into the English class system.

Cambridge may no longer be filled with 'Hooray Henrys'. The strangely dressed 'Trinity Foot' beaglers, scrambling without horses but in full hunting regalia across the countryside, may only survive as a pub sign on the busy A14 road. But vestiges remain and Cambridge undoubtedly still has a snobbish appeal and value to some as a sort of superior intellectual finishing school for young gentlemen and ladies.

ASSOCIATIONS

For the first seven of its eight hundred year history, the important collective entity in Cambridge was the College. In the later nineteenth century, science laboratories grew rapidly and provided an alternative magnet for students and staff. They have increased in strength and now Cambridge is in effect in three geographical locations. There is the old centre with its Colleges, some science Departments and laboratories and a few of the social science Departments. There is a newer site across the river Cam where various other arts and humanities and social science Departments and Faculties have moved, and there is a very substantial ring of large science laboratories and science parks round the edges of the city.

During the last hundred years, the balance of attraction has not only moved towards laboratory science, but also towards Faculties, Departments and Centres alongside the College.[1] This is a relatively recent phenomenon. Faculties were only instituted as formal entities in a revision of the Statutes of the University in

---

[1]Sometimes the bottom level of an organization is a Faculty—as with Law, Economics and History. In other cases, the Faculty is sub-divided into Departments, as with the Faculty of Archaeology and Anthropology, contained the Departments of Archaeology, Social Anthropology and Biological Anthropology.

1925 which were implemented in 1926.[2] The postgraduate students, who constitute much of their core, in particular the Ph.D. courses, are also recent, for it was only in 1919 that a Ph.D. degree was instituted at Cambridge.

These University entities now organize most of the teaching, all of the examining, and much of the research, yet surprisingly they have received little formal attention from analysts. While there have been many accounts of life in Cambridge Colleges, as far as I know no one has described in detail how the Departments and Faculties evolve and work. This is partly because many of these institutions have a pale and largely uninteresting bureaucratic existence, with only a limited communal identity or culture. As Rose and Ziman put it, they 'are often shadowy, sickly affairs . . . . They run no dances, no teas, no *conversazioni*. They do not even go in for Faculty photographs.'[3] This is true of a number of the large arts and social science institutions, such as the Faculties of History or Economics. And currently their existence is under further pressure by higher-level institutions as the power of Councils of Schools grows.

However, some of the smaller Departments, for example History and Philosophy of Science or Archaeology, do have both a strong history, intellectual coherence and a corporate personality. Just as certain science laboratories, most famously the Old Cavendish, developed customs and culture, so these small Departments attract commitment and loyalty. They give their members a sense of belonging to some kind of intellectual community—not as strong as a College for many of the students and staff, and always in tension with the Colleges, yet an important arena for teaching and research.

Another reason for the absence of descriptions of Departmental and Faculty organizations is that they are so varied. It is possible to

[2]This may seem very late, especially as titles such as Reader, and the existence of the Tripos, preceded the establishment of Faculties. Other bodies, for example Boards of Study, organized these offices and examination structures.

[3]Rose and Ziman, *Camford Observed*, 138.

give a generic description of 'a College' that tends to apply roughly to them all. In the case of these other institutions, a description of one cannot necessarily be applied to any other. Physically, socially, intellectually and organizationally they are hugely varied, as they are in terms of size and length of history.[4]

*

It is difficult to understand the relationship between the Colleges, Departments and Faculties and the particular nature of the latter. One way to bring out their distinctive features is through comparison. What are the differences between a College and a Department, and how do they overlap?

The Colleges are often old. Even when they are new, they tend to have spacious buildings, lawns and gardens. They also tend to remain roughly in the same place, sometimes for half a millennium or more. In all these respects a Department is different.

Taking as an example the Department of Social Anthropology, which I know best, it has no courtyard, just fronting onto Free School Lane and backing onto the New Museum Site, sharing both these spaces with other Departments and the general public. It has no Chapel, no bedrooms or other living accommodation for students or staff. It has no kitchens or grand dining hall. It has no playing fields or Department gardens. What it does have are some staff rooms, a seminar and lecture room, a library (in another building, shared with other Departments in the Faculty), a museum (likewise shared with archaeology), a small computing area, a common room and a few desks for Ph.D. students.

The Department is in comparison to many others quite compact and relatively stationary. It started as a separate Department in 1973 as a few rooms in Downing Street and then migrated in the mid-1970s, by way of a period in another building, to its present position

---

[4]There are only 31 Colleges, but over 300 'other institutions', from large Faculties to small committees and syndicates.

at the end of the Old Cavendish Laboratory. It has always been crowded and short of space, but the solid old building with its famous history has given a sense of history and identity which many of the sparkling buildings of the newly moved Departments and Faculties elsewhere lack. Like the Oxford Department of Anthropology, it feels old, distinguished and somewhat cosy, if cramped, on its four floors.

*

Colleges and Departments have different, though overlapping, functions. Colleges have a number of social functions which have no counterpart in the Departments. The only thing my Department does is arrange a sherry party for the new taught Master's students, and a drinks party for the entire Department, including new Ph.D. students, and visitors at the beginning of the academic year.

In terms of teaching, however, there is a complex overlap. Colleges are in charge of all the work of undergraduate admissions. Departments play no formal role in this, although many of their individual members are also involved in College admissions and the Faculty as a whole may try to encourage and co-ordinate admissions to their discipline through the Colleges. On the other hand, the primary role in the admission to taught Master's courses and the Ph.D. programmes are in the hands of the Department and Faculties, even though an accepted candidate also needs, in parallel, to be accepted by a College. It is possible for a candidate to be accepted by a Department but then fail to get a College place, which would effectively mean a rejection by the University.

*

In terms of undergraduate teaching, the central core, which is the weekly supervision, is in the hands of the College. Most of the actual supervisions, at least in the Arts, Humanities and Social Sciences, are done in Colleges. Alongside the supervisions, however, are seminars on particular themes, often one or two a week. These are arranged by the Department and held there. In Social Anthropology there are about twenty-four lectures per paper, and hence about 120 lectures for a student in a year. These are organized and given by the Department, and often held in a Department lecture room. The structure of the course, the syllabus and content and reading lists are also entirely in the hands of the Department.

All examinations, at every level, from the first year to the Ph.D. are in the hands of the Department. It appoints or recommends the names of examiners, sets and marks the examination scripts and grades the candidates into classes—only reporting the results to the Colleges.

Finally, research at the higher levels is distributed between Colleges and Departments. Colleges support research through research Fellowships, travel and other grants, providing rooms and libraries and encouraging discussion and interchange, especially between disciplines. In the arts, humanities and social sciences it is probably the case that much of the research is still done in the College, books being collected from libraries and taken to College rooms to work on. But in the sciences, most of the research is laboratory based and hence located in Departments and Faculties.

The complex overlaps between ancient Colleges and more recent Departments causes some friction when one side or the other feels its role is being infringed or neglected. The very rapid shift in balance—a hundred years ago almost entirely a Collegiate University, now pretty balanced, with a preponderance of the Departmental strength in the sciences, and Colleges in arts and humanities—has caused strains.

There is a tension of loyalty for students and especially for the staff, many of whom belong in some way to both Department and College. Yet having these two separate but overlapping spaces, two sets of support, two parallel intellectual and social worlds, seems to encourage creativity and to combine a disciplinary boundedness with an inter-disciplinary openness which is one of the features of Cambridge.

*

A number of the Colleges are quite large, complex and modestly wealthy. Consequently they have a number of more or less full-time officials, College officers, with their own staff. Most University Departments are much smaller and their functions more limited. There is a Head of Department and an Academic Secretary. Both these appointments are for a limited term. In recent years they have been paid positions, reflecting the increased burden of work to be undertaken. These jobs are carried on alongside teaching and research. There are also a series of smaller committees on which people serve for a while and then move on. The only instituted offices are of the support staff—administrative, financial, and technical.

The different nature of the organizational structure is shown by the nature of meetings. Weekly meetings of the core staff of the Department are largely functional and practical, they deal with teaching and research—with a little on finance, health and safety and other matters. Some of the business comes down from and goes up to the next level of the Faculty Board and Degree Committee, which represent the interests of all the departments. The Department meetings are usually fairly brief and business-like with the Head of Department steering the group through the agenda.

College meetings, especially those of all the Fellowship, the Governing Body, deal not only with teaching and research, but often also with many aspects of a student or Fellow's life—their food, housing, leisure activities and their rights and duties. Thus the meetings sometimes have the feeling of a family gathering. They can take much longer, with more interventions, disagreements and emotion. There is much more talk of 'we', of precedents, of morality and ethics.

The different nature of the organizations can also be seen by the way in which its leader is chosen. Although there are exceptions, on the whole the Head of a College is normally chosen by all the Fellows through a long and complex process ending with a solemn open vote in the chapel. The chosen person may remain in the post for up to ten years or more and is *ex-officio* Chair of most of the important committees.

The Departments are creations of the University and answerable to it. This means that the Head of Department is officially appointed by the University. The choice of this person may be informally made by members of the Department, but it has to be approved by the University. There are few internal political struggles of the kind that characterize the elections to Heads of Colleges and there is no formal ritual associated with the taking or leaving of office.

*

One source of the strength of many Colleges is that from their original foundation endowment, and then by way of gifts over their hundreds of years of existence, they have built up wealth. This is distributed in their buildings and properties scattered over England, in silver plate and wine cellars, in books and manuscripts and paintings, and in financial investments. They often have an endowment of some millions of pounds which provides part of their income, alongside fees from students, as well as profits from catering and hosting conferences. Of course they often have large expenses in the upkeep of old buildings. King's College Chapel and its various buildings can cost up to a million pounds a year, on average, to maintain.

A Department has no endowment apart from a few small trust funds which were set up by previous members and which give scholarships and grants to its students. It needs to maintain reasonable relations with two sets of institutions—the University, which passes on various funds to pay for overheads and stipends and wages—and the Research Councils and Foundations which give grants for some of its students and for research work by its staff. Obtaining this money is a constant struggle and the balancing of the books and reacting to sudden swings in Government policy on funding is not easy. Increasingly there has been devolution of responsibility and an ever-increasing stress on accountancy.

There are few ways in which a Department can increase its core funding apart from the occasional gift of a donor who may establish a new post or add a new building. It cannot charge for tours round its cramped territory, host large conferences or call on its alumni for substantial sums.

*

The Colleges create and sustain a sense of identity by the use of various symbols. Each College has a particular colour associated with it—King's is royal purple for example. This colour is incorporated along with a crest (when appropriate) into various other symbols— flags, College ties and scarves, headed notepaper, wall decorations. Colleges also have a Latin motto and statues and portraits of famous ancestors.

When we turn to the Department we find that the symbolic statement of community is weak. There is no crest, no special colour, no special headed notepaper with its own departmental heraldic device, no departmental ties, scarves, gowns or flags. The only statements that this is a Department are signs on the front and back door and sometimes photographs of former members.

Most Cambridge Colleges have published histories and the larger ones have several. These describe their foundation and subsequent history, famous events and illustrious ancestors and explain their architecture. The longer histories are often summarized into a small printed guide for visitors, often describing the library, chapel and other parts of the College that are open to them to view.

The Department usually has little corporate memory. There are a few lines about the Department and its history and functions in the printed and web introductions for students, but there is nothing in detail. It is usually difficult without much work to find out who learnt or taught in the Department, who were the Professors, who the benefactors, what the organization and the culture of the place is. Those who join it tend to learn little about the place which they occupy.

Whereas the oral myths and legends of a College, who said what to whom, who thought what where, scandals and triumphs, tend to be passed on from generation to generation, very little is passed on inside a Department. Most staff and students only know a few names of illustrious predecessors, mainly of the previous generation.

*

Because a College has traditionally been a total institution, where, often at an impressionable age and in magnificent surroundings, a young person passes three or more years, it can leave its imprint for life. Reunions of various kinds occur frequently, people bring their children and grandchildren to visit their old College. They may even leave money, furniture or a bench for the Fellow's Garden.

Even for the staff who stay in the Department for most of their working life, the Department does not often have the same pull. Nor does it attract the lifelong loyalty of undergraduates. Occasionally it may have some strong attachment for postgraduates who, for a few years, are often more closely bound to the Department than to their College.

As a consequence, few Departments produce an alumni magazine or newsletter. The names of the departed members tend to be forgotten, not merely the undergraduates and graduates, but even many of those who teach intensively for periods there. I have never met a proud father or mother showing their children or grandchildren round the Department. While I have been revisited by undergraduates I have taught in King's, never have they shown any interest in revisiting the Department.

*

Anthropologists have long discussed how difficult it is to get below the surface of a society—to see into the eddying currents which lie beneath the ripples. They have devised a number of techniques to reveal the normally hidden, including the 'social drama' approach. A fight, a quarrel and other moments of stress along with the discussion which often accompanies or follows them allow them to probe deeper.

Where are the revealing social dramas that take one to the depths of the social structure at Cambridge? In terms of the Colleges, it is in the election to the Headship. In relation to Departments, the election to an important Chair can be revealing. Parties and social events sometimes give clues, as do the discussions (and facial expressions) in Departmental seminars, in the weekly administrative meetings, and in gossip with one's friends. They can be seen in the annual process of working out the following year's teaching syllabus— lecture list planning meetings. In the past at these meetings there was obvious jockeying for power, quarrels over territory, hurt feelings of exclusion and the exercise of patronage.

The central and protracted annual cycle of examinations provides a repeated 'social drama' where some of the deeper alignments, tensions and battles momentarily come to the surface. None of the other meetings is as dramatic and extended as the four or five hours spent on the setting of exam questions, along with the many smaller meetings that go on around this, culminating in the meeting when the students are assigned a class—First, Upper Second and so on.

The amount of emotion here is higher than in any other event in the calendar. If there is a 'Cambridge cockfight' to be analysed, it is the metaphorical bloodletting of the examining process—the blood is partly that of colleagues wounded in the minor intellectual battles. Other 'blood' is that of students who, having been treated with equality are suddenly chopped into separate classes. Very quickly after they have graduated, the final year students are ejected from a place which they have probably come to love and feel part of, with a label ('II: 1' 'Third') stuck around their necks for the rest of their lives.

No wonder I always feel a mixture of a sense of relief and guilt after the final meeting. I feel as if I have been involved in an exciting chase. But when it is over, I am faced with the carcases I have slain lined up on a bench in front of me.

*

The brief analysis of some of the features of a Department in Cambridge could be paralleled by a similar analysis of the laboratories for which the University has become famous. In the back of my mind I have been aware of these since my Department is located in the most famous of these, the Old Cavendish Laboratory. These laboratories have often been little associational worlds where the intense competition and collaboration of a small number of people have led to extraordinary discoveries. As a nod in the direction of a vast array of important institutions, here is a glimpse of just one corner which I have come to know, in the way I came to know a couple of rooms in one Cambridge College.

In January 1975 I moved into a room on the top floor of a building in Free School Lane in Cambridge. At that time I knew nothing about Cambridge science. There were no indications that anything important had happened in any of the buildings there— though some appeared later. I pass these plaques every day. The one at the entrance reads:

Cavendish Laboratory 1874–1974
Established by the Duke of Devonshire and extended by Lord Rayleigh (1908) and Lord Austin (1940), the Cavendish Laboratory housed the Department of Physics from the time of the first Cavendish Professor James Clerk Maxwell until it moved to new laboratories in west Cambridge.

The other plaque notes that J.J. Thomson discovered the electron in this building, the foundation of most of modern electronics and computing.

Later I realized that I had come across a reference to the building once before. Reading in that oasis of civilization the British Council Library in what was then the very remote town of Pokhara in Nepal

Old Cavendish Laboratory

The entrance to the Old Cavendish Laboratory from Free School Lane, taken in the middle of the twentieth century. At the top of this tower the atom was split for the first time earlier work having taken place in the basement to what is now the Department of Social Anthropology. It was in the Old Cavendish that many scientists made their discoveries, including Maxwell (electromagnetism), Thomson (electrons), Dirac (dark matter), Chadwick (neutrons), Crick and Watson (DNA) and Hewish and Ryle (pulsars).

in 1969, I had read a description by the science journalist Nigel
Calder. He had explained how a rich American visitor had been
shown the cluttered rooms where a number of Nobel Prize winning
scientists were working with self-made, labour intensive machinery.
When he had offered to pay for a new laboratory, his guide had, in
a truly British way, said 'no thank you, for it is the very struggle that
helps us to achieve'. Later the scientists succumbed and the reason
I moved into part of the Old Cavendish in 1975 was because they
had relocated to the new West Cambridge site.

Over the years I have gathered scraps of gossip about the building
I work in. I relish stories of the Nobel Prize for radio astronomy
won in the rooms off the corridor at the top of our Department; of
Rutherford telling an excited young researcher that only when he
could explain his discovery to the barmaid of the local pub, the Eagle,
would it be worth something. I read accounts like Brian Cathcart's
The Fly in the Cathedral (2004), where the description of the almost
final phase of the work that led to the first splitting of the atom
appears to have occurred in the basement of our Department.

I heard with bemusement that the radioactivity caused by the
final work on establishing the atomic particles was only cleared up
some half century after the famous experiments. I lectured in the
Maxwell lecture room, apparently unchanged from the great days,
just as the lift which went up and down the tower where so much
happened is still there.

If anywhere in Cambridge exemplifies the way in which
concentrated, interdisciplinary work can occur within an apparently
ramshackle building, it is the Old Cavendish. Of course, we have
moved on from the era of sealing wax and string to that of computers
and gleaming instruments. Yet, for a few decades, mathematics,
physics, chemistry and a host of other disciplines came together in
this corner of a site which had once been a Benedictine monastery
and then a botanical garden.

Conveniently located close to two good pubs, the Bath (after
the medieval bath house) and the Eagle, a small group of scholars

worked on fundamental problems in various sciences. The massive effort required to perfect the Newtonian system and then to launch out into the surrealist world of quantum mechanics and physics was in no small part achieved here. Part of the work on many of the secrets of life on earth was done in this old building—the ultimate building blocks of all matter, the atom, the electron and neutron, the double helix of DNA. It fills me with awe.

*

Cambridge now has a ring of technology companies stretched round it, the largest such complex in Europe and reputedly the second largest in the world. These have grown up in the last thirty years and since I have been indirectly involved in several of these start-ups I have again been aware of how rich the proliferation of associational groupings have become. A number of them grew up directly out of the laboratories—computing, biology, and physics—and recruited the energies of students and staff. Many of their directors are also Fellows of Colleges and the associational nature of these dynamic groups is anchored in the older communities of Cambridge.

They started in the 1970s with the establishment of the Cambridge Science Park by Trinity College, later to be followed by St John's Science Park. They have been nurtured by a number of talented individuals and by the work of various University bodies. They now fit within other structures, such as the medical work done around the New Addenbrooke's site, in particular at the MRC laboratory for molecular biology, and the Judge Business School on the Old Addenbrooke's site. The turning of scientific discoveries into productive innovations and then into mass produced objects, the virtuous circle of creative innovation, is strongly encouraged and all our lives are being altered by this. The fact that many international firms, Olivetti, Microsoft and others have set up major research centres in Cambridge is another part of this phenomenon.

*

The Cavendish Laboratory and other laboratories and science Departments emerged to a large extent out of museums, as did my own Faculty of Archaeology and Anthropology. The first step was often to set up a Museum where objects were studied, as with geological, zoological or anthropological specimens. Out of these emerged teaching departments. The sites they are located on are known by names such as 'The New Museums Site', emphasizing the connection between laboratories and museums. The museums have been another set of associational bodies, bridging private research, preservation of great collections, and public outreach.

One of the most famous is the Fitzwilliam Museum, funded by Sir Richard Fitzwilliam, who endowed it with a marvellous collection of books and illuminated manuscripts, pictures and drawings and with £100,000 to build a house for them in 1816. The work was begun in the year the Victorian Era began, 1837; it was finished in the year of revolutions, 1848. Like the Museum of Geology, the Sedgwick Museum, the Museum of Archaeology and Anthropology, the Classical Museum, the Zoology Museum and the Whipple Museum of the History of Science, these are important enriching associational institutions.

Cambridge is also very rich in libraries in the Colleges, Faculties and in some Departments. At the centre is the University Library, one of the great libraries of the world. The library has medieval roots, but was expanded greatly during the later seventeenth century and after large gifts from George I it was moved to a new site in 1730. The building was substantially modified but the books kept arriving and it was finally moved to its new home across the river in 1935. The library now contains over seven million volumes. Because it is one of a select number of 'copyright' libraries, it receives free copies of all books published in the United Kingdom. It is also now obliged to take new forms of media, including digital materials, and has set up one of the first digital libraries, 'Dspace' or 'Digital Space', to archive this material.

In many libraries, most of the books are kept in locked stacks and one has to order them and wait for the book to arrive. This means that usually one has to know that a book exists before one finds it. One of the particular delights and sources of serendipity in the Cambridge library which, to my mind, more than compensates for the fact that it is less beautiful or well-endowed with books than the Bodleian Library at Oxford, is that much of it is 'open stack'. This means that when researching a new subject, one just has to find one or two initial books in the field, and then one will be taken to a set of shelves which have many other potentially useful books on them. These other works would not necessarily have been recovered by the very cleverest of library cataloguing systems.

Arranged around the University library are at least three rings of satellite libraries. One is the set of often magnificent and ancient College libraries, with their archives and rare collections, in particular that of Trinity College. Any one of the major libraries are equivalent to the whole library of a less fortunate University.

A second ring is the Faculty, Department and Institute libraries—many of them old and extremely well endowed with important works. They are usually more than just teaching libraries since they contain rare books and collections for research. Now that they are linked through a unified catalogue to the other libraries and to the University Library, they form a very substantial distributed library.

A third ring are area studies and special collections—the African, South Asian and other collections, not least amongst which is the impressive library of Chinese books based on the collection of Sir Joseph Needham at the Needham Centre. Each of these libraries has its own subculture, traditions, myths and sets of working relationships, often forming for students and staff a mini-world which they inhabit for intense periods.

The books in Cambridge libraries are supplemented by other institutions, in particular by the world famous University Press. Printing has been going on in Cambridge from the 1520s, and perhaps before, but a Royal Charter in 1534 gave the University the licence to name three printers who were allowed to print and publish approved works. Then in 1584 regular publication began under this privilege and there developed one of the oldest and largest continuous publishing houses in the world.

Alongside the publishing houses, Cambridge has traditionally been rich in bookshops. The most famous is perhaps Heffers, which has grown into a huge bookshop (no longer owned by the Heffer family). And for a long time David's second-hand bookshop, started in 1896, was the place where the great book-collectors of Cambridge such as John Maynard Keynes, Tim Munby and others used to visit to stock their collections. I was in Cambridge just early enough to know some of these collectors and to hear of their extraordinary finds on the barrow in the market to which the David family bought the fruit of London auctions. Other well-known bookshops include Galloway and Porter and have recently been joined by international chains such as Waterstone's and Border's. New media of various kinds may be supplementing books, but it is unlikely that the vast array of libraries and bookshops will cease to be important micro-associational institutions.

*

There are also numerous more informal and often ephemeral entities such as the rowing clubs and other sports clubs, choirs, debating societies and dramatic societies. A whole book could be written about this world, but I shall confine myself to one or two examples.

Cambridge is where many people start to find their special niche, aptitude, and enthusiasms. This is partly done through formal study, but equally through the myriad of activities which take up just as much time.

The many clubs and societies are funnels or doorways into new spaces, which may absorb a person's emotions and thoughts for a whole life. Cambridge is where a person can discover, at a serious level, what their real interests are and make the first important contacts with an outside, adult, world which will encourage them in these interests. Most vocational commitments require both enthusiasm and aptitude. At University you can discover if you have these.

It is not easy to convey the variety and richness of the world of clubs and societies. The official University list of registered clubs runs to more than three hundred, and there must be several hundred unregistered societies, such as the College drinking societies. Thus the twelve thousand or so undergraduates at any time in Cambridge have the choice of up to five hundred or more different organizations they can join.

To give an idea of the diversity, let me just list those under the letter 'S' on the University website:

Sakhya (Cambridge Friends of India), Scandinavian, Science Fiction, Science Productions, Scientific, Scout and Guide, Sedgwick, Self-Defence, Women's Selwyn Amateur Dramatics, Selwyn Jazz, Students in Free Enterprise, Sikh, Skydiving, Slavonic and East European, Slovenian, Social Anthropology, Social Documentary Film, Social Entrepreneurs, Southeast Asian Volunteers, Southern Africa Fund for Education, Southern Africa, Spaceflight, SPEAK, Spirit of the Cam, Sri Lanka, St Catherine's Music, Strathspey and Reel, Strong and Humorous Women, Student Action for Refugees, Student Alliance, Student Community Action, Student Green Belt, Student Law Review, Student Liberal Democrats, Student Pugwash Society, Student Run Computing Facility, Students Against the Arms Trade, Students Science Week Group, Students Supporting Street Kids, Surfing, Swing Band, Symphony Orchestra.

If none of the above attract one, there are many others, including the Amoral Sciences Club, Women's Belarusian Society, Women's Bobbin Lace-Making Club, Gog Magog Molly, Harry Potter Society (Society $9^3/_4$), Life Extension and Rejuvenation Society, Madhouse Theatre, Role Playing Society, Tiddlywinks Club and the Ultimate Frisbee Club.

Societies come and go, reflecting changing interests, and many of them have their own peculiar characteristics in terms of when and where they meet and their local customs. For example, in my College of King's, there was one which was formed by Lytton Strachey and Leonard Woolf among others called 'The Midnight

Society' which met on 'K' staircase on Saturdays at midnight in Clive Bell's rooms, a precursor of the Bloomsbury Group. Another was the 'Political Economy Club' which was founded by John Maynard Keynes, which professors, graduate students and some undergraduates were members of. This was not to be confused with the 'Political Society' which was, by the time I encountered it, meeting in the outer room of the set where I had a room (G2 in Gibbs). It was largely a historical society distinguished by its method of forcing people to ask questions in a random order by getting them to draw a number out of a bag.

One particularly intriguing society was the 'Cambridge Apostles', so-called because there were, at any one time, only twelve members. It seems important because it was the apex of the Cambridge system. Other clubs and societies took people out into the wider world. The Apostles were chosen from particularly promising undergraduates who looked as if they might turn into brilliant thinkers, writers and artists, some of whom would stay in Cambridge. It surrounded this process with secrecy and ritual. It was forbidden to talk about the membership or proceedings to others. It was something like a Masonic brotherhood and once a member there were lifetime obligations of support and intimacy.

It was a society which started as a *conversazione* or debating society nearly two hundred years ago. Over the centuries it had a considerable influence not only on its own members but also on wider British society through members such as Lord Tennyson, Henry Maine, F.W. Maitland, G.M. Trevelyan, Bertrand Russell, A.N. Whithead, J.M. Keynes, E.M. Forster, Ludwig Wittgenstein, G.H. Hardy, Leonard Woolf, G.E. Moore, Rupert Brooke, and others. More recently people like Peter Shore the politician, Jonathan Miller the polymath and the historian Quentin Skinner have been Apostles and it is still believed to be active, now with both women and men as members.

*

Somewhere at the intersection between clubs and institutions are the various dramatic and musical venues in Cambridge. There is a University concert hall as well as the famous Chapels, there are several theatres, including the oldest University playhouse, the ADC theatre, opened in 1855, and the Arts Theatre, established in the early twentieth century by John Maynard Keynes. Many young performers have made their first semi-professional appearances in such venues.

Each of these clubs and societies is a small sub-set of interests moving alongside other activities. Each has its own hierarchies, customs and laws and they only partially intersect. You can be top of one, but it does not necessarily have any particular impact on others. Thus it forms a mass of what some people call 'civil society', that is the middling forms of association which give our lives a meaning but are not created by the authorities.

These numerous associations have many effects. One is that it becomes impossible to generalize about the 'Cambridge experience'. Each person who passes through Cambridge follows a very different path, not merely because of the difference of academic subject, teachers, College life and informal friendship contacts, but because they spend much thought and emotion on other activities. This makes the writing of this book both more interesting and, ultimately, frustratingly personal, since each person will know a different Cambridge to that which I depict.

Another effect is to make Cambridge a very busy place. When I asked a third-year anthropology student what she thought was the most striking feature of Cambridge, she said that it was that time was so precious, and timetabling so important. She felt a constant anxiety about time and not wasting it. There was so much to do, and so little time. There was a constant sense of speed, hurry, no time for mistakes. She could not afford to be ill—there is too much to do. She found herself furious if people failed to show up, were late, wasted her 'precious time'. All this came into sharp relief when she went away from Cambridge and time suddenly slowed down and instead of there being too much to do and too little time, it was often the reverse.

*

The proliferation of numerous bodies in Cambridge which call on people's allegiance, efforts and commitment, but which does not overwhelm them in a mindless loyalty, is the background to a certain strand of thought. At the time when the older, Collegiate, communal, system was being challenged by these new associations, in the century after the 1850s, a number of important thinkers in Cambridge reflected deeply on the nature of the relationship between community and association and the problems of pluralistic systems. It is perhaps not too much to suggest that their daily experience negotiating these great changes helped to give them experience and an interest in a transformation to what many have thought of as one central characteristic of the modern world.

Very briefly, this background nurtured the ideas of one of the seminal thinkers in this area, Sir Henry Maine, Professor at Cambridge and Master of Trinity Hall, who from the 1850s onwards wrote extensively on what, in his most famous phrase, he called 'the movement of the progressive societies from status to contract'. In other words, the movement from bonds based on birth, blood, community, to those based on choice, contract and association. His ideas fit exactly with the difference between Colleges and other institutions.

His vision was deepened and qualified by his successor, F.W. Maitland. He saw that modern societies are filled with mixtures of status and contract. Maitland's ideas on the importance of Trusts and trust, of the pluralism of allegiances which give individual freedom mixed with collaboration, was further elaborated in the first half of the twentieth century by a Cambridge political theoretician F.N. Figgis. Figgis argued, for example, that 'the real question of freedom in our day' is not the rights of the individual but 'the freedom of smaller unions to live within the whole'.[5] In a parallel fashion, the political theorist Michael Oakeshott centred his work on similar themes and described as his ideal an associational world which is an almost direct description of the multitudinous associations of Cambridge.[6]

It thus seems that Cambridge over the last century and a half has been a living experiment in how to nurture and regulate civil society, that is the balance of delegated power that leads to freedom with responsibility. It is in such a world that people can effectively balance what Adam Smith called 'self love' and 'social love', the drive to succeed and win and the desire to be appreciated and work with others. The extraordinary flourishing of Cambridge in the twentieth century must surely be related to this complex and heterogeneous social structure. The dangers of too much community introversion, as had emerged in the Colleges by the early nineteenth century, has been countered by the associational proliferation, which has not become arid and over-competitive precisely because it is in turn balanced by the College system.

[5]Goldie in Mason (ed.), *Cambridge Minds*, 187.
[6]In Mason (ed.), *Cambridge Minds*, 234.

IDEAS

The Bath House at Night

The Bath referred to in the name was the bath house of the Augustinian monastery which stood on this spot for several centuries. Like other pubs and coffee houses it has been a centre of the relaxed and playful speculative talk which has encouraged people to see the world in a new way.
[Photograph: courtesy Zhiguang Yin]

The Eagle Pub at Night

The pub is well known as one of the grand old coaching inns of Cambridge and as the place where in February 1953 Francis Crick announced to his friends at the back of the pub that they had worked out the helical structure of DNA, 'the secret of life'.
[Photograph: courtesy Zhiguang Yin]

EDUCATION

It is easy to overlook the real purpose of Cambridge, that it is a place of learning, an intellectual institution. It is defined, in the oath which new Fellows take at King's as a place of 'religion, education, learning and research'. Cambridge is a centre where ideas are generated, contested and disseminated, where the tools to create and to discover are made and passed on. By most measures it has been effective, both at the level of the students who pass through it and those who do research here.

Yet it is particularly difficult to describe this central activity. If we accept that to educate means something more than passing on information, then it is largely experienced in a struggle to absorb, reshape and transmit ideas which cannot be reduced to formal book learning. Furthermore, each teacher has a different experience and methods. Yet without this dimension, surprisingly so often missing in books about Cambridge, the rest is meaningless.

I shall attempt to sketch a little of this world of learning by drawing on parts of my own experience. This may have the virtue of making the account more concrete, even if it also makes it less widely applicable.

*

Cambridge is an old University living in the modern world and its early origins, like that of other European universities, have given it a special oral flavour. For the first quarter of a millennium after its founding there was no printing in the western world and hence everything had to be transmitted orally or on parchment. Most teaching was by verbal transmission from Master to Pupil—through personal apprenticeship one became a Master of Arts. This was done in two main ways, by lecturing and by personal one-to-one teaching.

Formally I am expected to do a certain number of lectures a year; for a university lecturer in the arts, humanities and social sciences the norm is not less than around forty a year. Thus in my years in Cambridge I have given over a thousand one-hour lectures, each of which requires considerable preparation.

The diversity of the lectures we are expected to do can be seen from a small sample of the major lecture series I have given. For the first year students I have lectured on kinship and marriage, on an introduction to anthropology, on political and economic anthropology, war, famine and disease and long-term transformations in civilizations. In the second and third years, on classical theories in the social sciences, theories of the state, technology, property, visual anthropology, feudalism and capitalism, legal anthropology, violence and war, urban anthropology, inequality, population, the history of the family, sexual behaviour, cosmologies of capitalism and research methods.

As well as the formal lectures, we are expected to hold seminars for ten to twenty students who take turns to present papers. These occur at all levels of the course. The art is to encourage, bring out, and arbitrate, without intervening too much. A good seminar is a really exciting event.

This constant engagement in the rather strange process of making ideas clear and interesting through oral delivery has numerous effects. It forces me to work out what I really think. It stimulates me to range more widely and generally than if I just based lectures on my own research. Like all teachers, I find it is stressful and sometimes dispiriting.

Undergraduates are not forced to attend any lectures, so they only come if they feel it is helpful. That many do learn in this essentially medieval way is an indication that lectures are still, after all these centuries, a useful way to find out what is currently happening in various intellectual worlds.

*

The current College-based supervision (tutorial) system is a late nineteenth century development, evolving out of an eighteenth century system of private tuition.[1] 'In 1902 the *Student's Handbook* announced that there was no need for most students to seek private tuition, as College, intercollegiate and professorial teaching were quite sufficient.'[2] The best College teachers, borrowing from the best tutors, revived the system of question and answer which had dated from medieval times.

The supervisions occur about once a week during full term. Usually each student or pair of students is given four to six supervisions per paper. The student prepares some work, an essay or equivalent. The supervisor has set the topic and proceeds to ask questions and make comments. It can be highly rewarding and exciting, or, sometimes, less than helpful and even embarrassing.

Many of my best ideas have been worked out with students, yet both the supervisions themselves and often the reading of the essays before and afterwards take a great deal of effort. As Rose and Ziman note, 'to be successful a tutorial usually demands a constant and very carefully controlled projection of personality on the part of a supervisor. It requires great expenditure of nervous energy . . . .'[3] The teaching requires a mixture of criticism and confidence boosting. Arthur Benson noted that 'I realised . . . that generous and simple

---

[1]The changes are well described in Sheldon Rothblatt, *The Revolution of the Dons* (Cambridge, 1968), 207ff.

[2]ibid., 234.

[3]Rose and Ziman, *Camford Observed*, 153.

praise, outspoken encouragement, admiration, directness, could win victories that no amount of strictness or repression could win. I began to see that enthusiasm and interest were the contagious things . . .'[4] the effects of this approach are described by the musician Raymond Leppard when writing of his tutor. 'As a teacher, he had that greatest gift of all of making you feel that he thought you so much better than you knew you were; and you loved him, so you couldn't let him down by not being so.'[5]

During my time in Cambridge I have supervised well over two hundred undergraduates. I have done so in almost every field of social anthropology, from politics to religion, from theory to method, from first to third years. It is difficult to explain what goes on in these intense sessions.

Rose and Ziman describe the variety of settings. 'What are tutorials like? It is almost impossible to say. They are as different as each don, each undergraduate who goes to make them. Some last for several hours, conversation coming in odd bursts while the don dresses, fries an omelette, sings snatches of Italian opera, dusts the knick-knacks on the mantelpiece. Some start and stop dead upon the hour and are marmoreally silent banquets of the mind. Some take place in panelled, gilded chambers where one sits on antique chairs sipping sherry and eyeing priceless works of art. Some take place in sparsely furnished offices with metal filing cabinets standing shivering in the corners.'[6]

As for the essay, we are told that 'Some like to receive them at the beginning of the tutorial hour and sit silently reading, emitting terrifying coughs while the undergraduate tries to see in their faces how things are going. At the end of three-quarters of an hour the don will hand back the manuscript, perhaps murmuring laconically: "Very nearly", or "Rather too rich" or "Yes, I think so". Some

[4]Benson, *College Window*, 132.
[5]Hayman (ed.), *My Cambridge*, 106.
[6]Rose and Ziman, *Camford Observed*, 69.

dons get the undergraduates to read their essays out loud. The undergraduate declaims the first sentence. In breaks the don with admiration and expostulation. He launches into diatribes, harangues, exhortations. By the end of the tutorial the essay is forgotten as he argues heatedly with himself . . . .' Many people get a great deal out of the tutorials as they learn to argue and to sift evidence, 'They learn to discuss intellectual topics freely, fairly and penetratingly. Weekly contact with an older person who is sympathetic yet not too intimate eases them into the problems and perturbations of the adult world.'[7] Others find them unhelpful and even absurd.

The author Christopher Isherwood remembered reading out his first essay to 'the dreaded Mr Gorse'.

'The subject of the essay was: "Better England Free than England Sober". I had finished it with some pride: it exactly suited my idea of Mr Gorse's requirements—snappy, epigrammatic, a bit daring in its language, sprinkled with witticisms borrowed unacknowledged from Mr Holmes [his previous schoolteacher]. Only now, for some reason, all my effects seemed to have gone wrong: the verbal fireworks were damp; the epigrams weren't epigrams but platitudes, pompous, painfully naïve, inept and priggish. It was positive misery to have to utter them. I writhed with embarrassment, coughed, made spoonerisms.'

As Isherwood read the last paragraph Gorse started to drum his fingers on the mantelpiece.

'"Yes, yes . . ." he kept muttering: "Yes, yes . . ." as though his impatience were increasing with every word. "Well", he told me, when, at last, I had finished: "I'll say this for you—it's not the work of an entirely uneducated fool". He paused. I grinned hopelessly; regarding him like a poodle which is going to be kicked. "Look here, Isherwood," he appealed to me abruptly, "don't you yourself agree that it's all tripe?"'[8]

[7]Rose and Ziman, *Camford Observed*, 70.
[8]Christopher Isherwood, *Lions and Shadows* (Signet edn., 1974), 37.

Of course this is at the 'eccentric' end. Most of those I experienced as a student were more sober—and, for me at least, more useful. There is often an atmosphere of experiment, of trying out ideas, of realizing that the way one says things is as important as what one says, that, as one of my teacher's put it, 'one fruitful error is worth a thousand stale truths'.

*

A good deal of the system of trying to assess quality through written exams was invented in Cambridge. For example, we are told that the concept of grading students' work quantitatively was developed by a tutor named William Farish at Cambridge in 1792.[9] The University set up its Local Examination Syndicate in 1858. This Syndicate, Cambridge Assessment, is the largest such agency in Europe. The Oxford and Cambridge Schools Examination Board now sets the standards of exams around much of the world.

Medieval examinations were oral disputations 'in which the candidates advanced a series of questions or theses which they disputed or argued with opponents a little senior to themselves, and finally with the masters who had taught them.'[10] By the eighteenth century those who had completed the first stage of their graduation were arranged in order of merit. At the graduation ceremony a senior BA, sitting as a licensed fool on a three-legged stool or tripod, read out entertaining verses at the ceremony, so that these were known as the Tripos. More specifically, the Tripos came to mean the examination in mathematics, which by 1800 was a written examination.

The Cambridge system has remained particularly strict. In my subject, no elements of the coursework—the weekly essays or projects—are allowed to count in the final examinations. Only in the third year does the dissertation (which is optional and usually done by about two thirds of the cohort) count as one fifth of the

[9]According to *Wikipedia* 'University of Cambridge'.
[10]History of the University on the University website.

marks. Such a system puts a high premium on memory, stamina, and rapidity of thought, ingenuity and writing skills. It has many advantages. It is less open to abuse than assessed coursework modules; it is a better test of real understanding and, I think, superior to multiple-choice and other methods used in some universities. Quite often there are essays of great brilliance which astonish me. Yet it is indeed stressful for the students and in another way for the markers.

The whole process is anonymous and the candidates are ascribed their classes without being named. Later the names are revealed—to the occasional acclamation or expression of disappointment. The Cambridge system is impersonal. From the start to the end all you are judging is the person's intellect in a three-hour session. Nothing else counts. The Cambridge system gives justice between candidates and between years. Favouritism, chance and special knowledge do not help.

*

Until two generations ago, nearly all the teaching in Cambridge revolved around undergraduates. Increasingly, however, much more of what goes on concerns postgraduates, both those on taught Master's courses and doctoral research, who now constitute about one third of the students at Cambridge. Again, how this is organized and what happens varies hugely between disciplines and individuals.

I have supervised over forty Ph.D. students in my time in Cambridge, on average five to ten at any one time. They have worked on almost every imaginable topic in almost all parts of the world. Here are a few examples: 'broadband' in China, whitening of the face in Japan, family structures in Singapore, religion in Sarawak, social change in Vietnam, identity in Malaysia, shamanism in Nepal, hunter-gatherers in India, development in South America, tourism in Greece, politics in Spain, nationalism in Germany, manufacturing in France, kinship in England and farming in Ireland.

My approach to this intense relationship with another human being over a number of years is to try to maintain a high level of interest in what they are doing, speedy responses to any theoretical or practical problems, some general advice on writing and suggestions on bibliographical and other resources and above all constant encouragement in the lonely task of writing. It is again a privilege and a responsibility. While something like a quarter of my intellectual energy over my time in Cambridge has been devoted to postgraduate supervision and examining, it is a rewarding process for the supervisor as well. I have learnt a great deal and many of my former students have become distinguished in their own fields and remained friends.

*

The official side of education in Cambridge is nowadays very demanding for both the teachers and the students. As the pressures on the formal side of the University teaching syllabus grows, it is worth remembering that education is about much more than what we learn explicitly in lectures, seminars or supervisions.

In *The Education of Henry Adams* we are reminded of the wider role of education outside the lecture room, and of the invisible ways in which ideas and approaches are passed on between generations. 'A parent gives life, but as parent, gives no more. A murderer takes life, but his deed stops there. A teacher affects eternity; but he can never tell where his influence stops . . . . He makes of his scholars either priests or atheists, plutocrats or socialists, judges or anarchists, almost in spite of himself.'[11]

John Raven in the 1930s put it in another way. If we take away the pipes and turn the men into men or women and set the scene in many different places, only one of them a cosy fireside, his description still rings true today. 'It is commonly supposed that boys go up to Cambridge in order to acquire knowledge from dons or laboratories; or to row and run . . . the secret of their work is not found in the lecture room or the playing fields or the Union Society or the dining club. Two men, two chairs, two pipes and a fire—that

[11]Henry Adams, *Novels, Democracy, Esther* (1983), 994.

is their symbol; and those nights of the gods when we rambled over all things in heaven and earth . . . . It is the vast and essential business of ranging oneself, of coming to terms with the universe, of discovering a purpose in life that the university exists to foster.'[12]

The essence is to combine many techniques, formal, semi-formal, informal, to help people find themselves. It is risky and often fails. It is easily destroyed by obsession with the official side. It requires constant nurturing. Yet, as we read the accounts of many of those who have passed through Cambridge and as I look back at my own career as an undergraduate and graduate at Oxford, I recognize the description by Raymond Leppard. 'There scarcely seemed time to draw breath and yet, somewhere within the frenetic energy of term, there lay the essence of the paradox that is the strength of the Oxbridge system. While we stretched ourselves to the limit, there was still time to find out about ourselves, our minds, our capabilities and failing—not all, but enough, at least, to make a good start.'[13]

Education is a total business, of head, heart, spirit and body, to use the old terms. This is why in describing Cambridge I have spent a great deal of time trying to capture something of the customs, culture, architecture and rhythms of Cambridge. These are just as important as the formal educational system.

*

It is difficult to assess the effects of Cambridge or what it has contributed to later achievements. Many of those who might be counted as 'Cambridge' products were in the University only for a few years. Many reacted against it while they were there and others disowned it for various reasons. Very many did their major work, whether as scientists, humanists or artists, after they left the University.

All that one can do is to infer indirectly. Many of those whom I have interviewed have stressed that the intellectual and emotional

---

[12]Lindsay, *Scrapbook*, 72, quoting C.E. Raven, *A Wanderer's Way* (1928).
[13]Leppard in Hayman (ed.), *My Cambridge*, 111.

atmosphere of Cambridge, has had a deep, if often indirect, effect throughout their life. This is true of my experience at Oxford. I suspect that if I had gone into a job unrelated to universities I would have continued to be aware that, like my early years in my family, I have been moulded to a considerable extent by the experience.

One way in which the influence works is nebulous, consisting in the feeling that one is treading in the footsteps of predecessors who have climbed the heights of creativity. Both Wordsworth and Tennyson wrote poems on visiting Milton's mulberry tree in Christ's, and Wordsworth in the *Prelude* wrote about the pleasure of being where Chaucer, Spenser and Milton had composed some of their poetry.

Rose and Ziman put the experience well. 'Even without a Fellowship, Oxford or Cambridge is a good place to be. They are not merely great and famous Universities. They are *The Universities*. They are significant elements in the whole Anglo-Saxon heritage. They are places of high magic, like Glastonbury and Stonehenge. To a spirit of any sensibility, it is a privilege, and a challenge, to walk where Newton walked, to teach where Erasmus taught, to preach where Cranmer or Newman preached, to master it where Jowett or Bentley was Master. The *genius lociorum* cannot be denied.'[14]

Switching to the effect on character and intelligence they comment that 'It comes, perhaps, from the feeling one has, as a freshman, of entering into the inheritance of a harmonious and undisturbed tradition of independence, tolerance, and respect for the human intelligence ... that one owes life a return. It comes most of all, perhaps, from the invitation to be oneself, and to explore the world in one's own way, with the help of one's friends, and only a little gentle mockery from one's seniors when one makes silly, foreseeable mistakes.'[15]

Throughout my time in Cambridge there have been signs of excitement and talk of new achievements. I may not have experienced this quite as intensely as C.P. Snow but I have certainly sensed it.

[14]Rose and Ziman, *Camford Observed*, 131.
[15]ibid., 246.

Snow, writing of the year 1932, comments that 'one could not help picking up the human, as well as the intellectual, excitement in the air. James Chadwick, grey-faced after a fortnight of work with three hours sleep a night, telling the Kapitsa Club . . . how he had discovered the neutron; P.M.S. Blackett . . . showing plates which demonstrated the existence of the positive electron; John Cockcroft, normally about as much given to emotional display as the Duke of Wellington, skimming down the King's Parade and saying to anyone whose face he recognized: "We've split the atom! We've split the atom!"'[16]

It is equally difficult to capture the emotional excitement, often with the first serious love affairs or friendships. There are moments of intense feeling which may last a lifetime. For example Vladimir Nabokov, who came to Trinity as a student in 1919 after his family fled the Russian Revolution, wrote, 'I remember the dreamy flow of punts and canoes on the Cam, the Hawaiian whine of phonographs slowly passing through sunshine and shade and a girl's hand gently twirling this way and that the handle of her peacock-bright parasol as she reclined on the cushions of the punt which I dreamily navigated. The pink-coned chestnuts were in full fan; they made overlapping masses along the banks, they crowded the sky out of the river, and their special pattern of flowers and leaves produced a kind of *en escalier* effect, the angular figuration of some splendid green and old-rose tapestry . . . . The three arches of an Italianate bridge, spanning the narrow stream, combined to form, with the help of their almost perfect, almost unrippled replicas in the water, three lovely ovals. In its turn, the water cast a patch of lacy light on the stone of the intrados under which one's gliding craft passed.'[17]

*

Most people's feelings about Cambridge, including my own, are mixed. Yet nearly always there is recognition that in some ways it

[16]C.P. Snow, *The Variety of Men* (Penguin, 1969), 11.
[17]Nabokov, *Speak Memory*, 208.

has changed our life. If we take just four who later excelled in different fields and who wrote about their experiences after the Second World War, we can glimpse some of the intense emotions Cambridge generates.

The literary critic and socialist Raymond Williams wrote that 'as I look across the fields to this strange city it is both easy and difficult to remember how much has happened to me here, and how important, at different times, it has been in my life. Easy because I still work here, with certain traceable continuities, and with so many places reminding me of past and present. Difficult because, over all these years, it still seems no more than an intersection; never a possession, of or by.'[18]

The economist John Vaizey wrote 'Cambridge did not make me. The pattern of neurosis I brought with me was not altered. I brought, too, the habit of work from hospital. But Cambridge formed me. It made me determined to be a don in order not to lose the way of life. That way of life was my introduction to adult life.'[19] He writes further that 'It is impossible for me, therefore, to look back on Cambridge calmly, or without a sense of its having in some sense been a limiting as well as a supremely liberating experience.'[20] It is a jumble of emotions. 'Nostalgia, reminiscence, forgetfulness, despair—these are the emotions conjured up and, as with a conjuror's trick, there is a feeling that, in a flash of movement too quick for the eye to register, the true experience has been missed.'[21]

The poet Tom Gunn wrote of the magic of performing The Taming of the Shrew in a College Garden: 'In the last scene as night came on, the servants held up flaming torches. It was Cambridge at its sweetest—Shakespeare, the moonlit summer night, the park-like private gardens of wealthy Colleges, friends I hoped would be friends

[18]Hayman (ed.), My Cambridge, 70.

[19]ibid., 124–5.

[20]ibid., 130.

[21]ibid., 132.

for life—different kinds of happiness rolled into one.' It was a fantasy place. 'Yet there was no fixed Cambridge. There was instead a number of beautifully kept-up old buildings and a core of teachers and retainers. This was a background against which a lot of intelligent young people improvised their fantasies of what "Cambridge" might be.'[22] He concludes, 'So I am grateful to Cambridge for many things. It enriched my life enormously, it gave me the security and advantages that everybody ought to have, but it also brought me up against someone who could eventually teach me that the real business was elsewhere completely.'[23]

The actress Eleanor Bron points to something which I also experienced, namely that the influence began many years before one even arrived. 'At school Cambridge and Oxford had been presented as absolutes, almost tangible values. Each word seemed to contain continuing and complex experience, to be almost as big as the big insufficient words like Marriage, Pain, Death . . . . In fact, as I see now, what my teachers were holding out to me were the golden globes of opportunity.'[24] Once Bron arrived at the University, the combination of the aesthetic and social had a deep effect: 'the physical beauty of Cambridge, the historic buildings of great grace and elegance, the river, the backs, smothered with daffodils in spring, all this, combined with the closeness of the society, could not help but contribute to the powerful impact of the place on its inmates. So many of them, inevitably, were at a particularly open moment of their lives, momentarily poised like passengers in an unusually well-appointed transit lounge.'[25]

The intensity and some of the spirit of what Cambridge education aims at is caught by a comment sent to me by a first-year student after he had been in Cambridge for three months. He

[22]ibid., 144.
[23]ibid., 148.
[24]ibid., 171–2.
[25]ibid., 186.

wrote that students should be told that in a subject such as anthropology their certainties would be challenged and they would be taught to doubt.

'I came to Cambridge and had a relatively fixed set of values, beliefs and convictions—not just in politics and religion, but relating to most spheres of social and public life, the world I live in. Cambridge education, however, makes the utmost effort to completely dismantle and deconstruct all thoughts and ways of thinking you have before you arrive. Everything is questioned, nothing is certain, and in the end I sit in my cosy room, thinking how little I have known and how ill-informed my judgments were. But nonetheless happy. All my cognitive processes, seeking order in the world surrounding me and striving to maintain certainty, are overwhelmed by the flow of information which leaves me wiser than before, but also so much less secure . . . . For me, this is the most interesting time of my life. Every day enhances thinking and knowledge considerably. What I have learned is that there are no straightforward answers. A claim to knowledge which appears certain and proven is often merely simplistic. There are no easy solutions. Life and the world in which it takes place are incredibly complex.'[26]

It is because of this intensity, and its often transitory nature, that many people feel unease about revisiting a place which is so full of powerful ghosts of their former self. 'Here spectres abound and the situation becomes more clear. Here there are streets and corners haunted forever: an unexpected meeting in the fog, a chase by the Proctors . . . .' Revisiting the library in Newnham, Bron observes 'I could not believe that I had ever sat there reading books, trying to think. It was like having spare memories, an uncanny sensation and not a very pleasant one: *not* seeing a ghost. Not seeing a ghost because you are the ghost.'[27] She claims that it did not teach

---

[26]I am very grateful to Jan-Jonathan Bock for permission to quote from this comment made in 2008.

[27]Hayman, My *Cambridge*, 172.

her to think, 'but it did light up new forks in the road and, directly and indirectly, gave me some of the people I love most in the world.'[28]

Perhaps, for those who are fortunate in their experience, E.M. Forster best puts the fusion of the elements. 'As Cambridge filled up with friends it acquired a magic quality. Body and spirit, reason and emotion, work and play, architecture and scenery, laughter and seriousness, life and art—these pairs which are elsewhere contrasted were there fused into one. People and books reinforced one another, intelligence joined hands with affections, speculation became a passion, and discussion was made profound by love.'[29]

Often it is only in rare moments that a person expresses the deep debt that many owed to Cambridge. One of the most moving is when the Cambridge theologian and Protestant martyr Nicholas Ridley wrote his farewell in October 1555, shortly before he was taken to be burnt at the stake for refusing to convert to Catholicism.

'Farwel therefore Cambridge, my loving mother and tender Nurse . . . . Thou didst bestow on me all thy school degrees, the common offices, the chaplainship of the University, the office of the Proctorship and of a common Reader, and of thy private commodities and emoluments in Colledges what was it thou madest me not partner of? . . . Farewell Pembroke Hall . . . . In thy orchard (the walls buts and trees, if they could speak would bear me witness) I learned without book almost all Pauls Epistles, yea, and I ween all the Canonical epistles . . . . The Lord grant that this zeal and love toward that part of God's word, which is a key and a true commentary to all the holy scriptures, may ever abide in that colledge so long as the world shall endure.'[30]

---

[28]Hayman, *My Cambridge*, 190.
[29]E.M. Forster, *Goldsworthy Lowes Dickinson*, (Arnold, 1934), 35.
[30]Quoted in Leedham-Green, *University of Cambridge*, 53.

CREATIVITY

'Far out in the uncharted backwaters of the unfashionable end of the Western Spiral arm of the Galaxy lies a small unregarded yellow sun. Orbiting this at a distance of roughly ninety-two million miles is an utterly insignificant little blue green planet whose ape-descended life forms are so amazingly primitive that they still think digital watches are a pretty neat idea.' One of those primitive life forms was a certain Cambridge University alumni, Douglas Adams, the author of the celebrated *Hitchhiker's Guide to the Galaxy* from which this passage is taken.

Adams might have continued thus. 'For most of human history, no one on this remote and insignificant planet paid much attention to the small wet island on the western edge of the backward end of the Eur-Asian continent. Gradually this island filled up with tribal peoples who only a little over a thousand years ago became the English. Remote and insignificant as England was, one of its poorest and most impenetrable areas was the marshy fenland of Cambridgeshire. Here, by chance, a group of monkish figures developed a centre of learning.'

The strangeness is that over a period of eight hundred years this tiny speck on a tiny planet became arguably the most important single centre for intellectual discoveries in history. Its scientists laid out many of the laws of the natural and physical world. How has an experiment in trying to answer the question of 'the meaning of life, the universe and everything' been so relatively successful? What are the sources of creativity, not only in the sciences but also in the arts, humanities and social sciences?

*

All human beings start with a creative potential, that is with a mixture of curiosity, wonder, a desire to experiment, to solve puzzles, to try out new things, to explore their world and to invent new solutions to make their life more enjoyable. Yet in the majority of societies such creativity is often constrained. Usually, the pressure of the State, religion and the family are brought to bear on the individual to inhibit more than a very limited creativity. Minor creative acts are sometimes tolerated or even encouraged, but deep creative attempts to change the world are almost always regarded as a threat.

The educational system, both at school and at University is very often an obstacle to creative thought. As Einstein put it, 'the only thing that interferes with my learning is my education.' Teachers very often rely on rote learning, respect for received opinions and the wisdom of ancestors. There is a strong hostility to deviations from the orthodoxy.

Though there are moments of creativity everywhere, yet when I think of my own experience at Cambridge, I detect something unusual. There are a series of what are sometimes known as 'paradigm shifts', deep discoveries which alter the way we look at the world, from Bacon and Newton to Maxwell and Crick and Watson. It seems that the often lonely, isolated, implausible, somewhat frightening pursuit of the deep mysteries of man and the natural world somehow flourished here.

This happened in the long struggle to find answers to the mysteries of science and arts at the level of advanced research. It was also encouraged for undergraduates. Whatever the inhibitions on creativity, repression of 'swots' and hard workers at school, at Cambridge all aspects of a person's creative potential are encouraged. Whatever they enjoy and are good at—games, music, acting, poetry and science.

During my six years as an undergraduate and postgraduate at Oxford, and my nearly forty years at Cambridge I have enjoyed this supportive and encouraging atmosphere. On the other hand, it is worth remembering that others experience less supportive conditions, including destructive conversation and obstacles from entrenched interests.

Nor have I ever felt that my more bizarre and outlandish attempts to discover new ways to pursue problems have been disapproved of by my colleagues. As a historian in a Department of anthropologists, as someone with a fascination with technologies (computers, videos) in a largely non-technological subject, I have found it unnecessary to fight for or justify my eccentricities.

It is a great spur as well as a pleasure to be esteemed in whatever one attempts to do, on the assumption that though it may look absurd at present, it may lead to something worthwhile and original. This encouragement of innovative thought is something I try to extend to my students. If they come up with exciting, if superficially implausible, ideas, I try to give them space and support to develop these. Better to try and to learn by one's errors than be constantly warned off difficult paths.

Originality is among the most highly esteemed qualities in academic life and has been for many years the main criterion for the award of a doctorate. To find out something new, to create an object that has never existed before, to find a new path round an old difficulty or to open up a new seam of knowledge, these are the highest goals. The whole of Cambridge University can be seen as an intellectual machine dedicated to creativity. Paradoxically Cambridge can be so partly because it is outwardly such a conservative and safe place.

The relative equality of formal ranking in the University, the absence of a sharp difference between research and teaching, the emphasis on esteem rather than formal position, all encourage creativity. The worst of reputations is to be thought dull. Lively, playful, probing but non-destructive conversation is encouraged.

Academic life can quickly degenerate into a zero sum game, of 'limited good', of 'frogs in a well' each scrabbling to hold the others down. The success of a colleague can be a bitter blow, encouraging backbiting and gossip, attempts to damage other's reputations, cliques and rivalries.

I may be unobservant but I have noticed relatively little of this in Cambridge. Private success is genuinely thought to lead to public benefit. The amount of reflected glory in the success of one's colleagues outweighs a private sinking feeling that they show up one's lack of success. It is like a good family, the parents rejoice in the success of their children and *vice versa*, rather than being threatened by it.

Cambridge has not given in to the pressure, which some other universities have succumbed to, of dividing staff into 'research active' and 'teachers only'. Indeed the deepest difficulty facing many universities, where what one is paid to do (teach) and what one gets prestige and promotion from (research) are in opposition, is largely absent. Good teachers are valued and are also encouraged to be good researchers.

The system gives space to eccentric genius. Over the years I have felt myself occasionally carrying the burden of supporting a colleague who might be thought to be a 'free rider', a hopeless committee person, refusing to do humdrum teaching and not very dependable. Yet they are also known to be brilliant, original and quirky. They are part of the glory of the place. For it is recognized that to achieve something really outstanding, to be a Newton, J.J. Thomson, Paul Dirac or Fred Sanger may not fit a person easily into the normal niceties of academic life. It may go with shyness, poor lecturing skills, a child-like innocence, and a great deal of obsessive selfishness.

The essence of creativity is that it requires mental and social space. A person or group needs the self-confidence, long and deep attention to clues, lack of fear of authority, to be able to challenge a current paradigm. To have an institution which has, to a considerable extent provided the context for such an unusual type of endeavour over a period of eight hundred years might be considered extremely unlikely. That Cambridge has managed to avoid the routinization and pressures to conformity which so easily invade an institution is indeed surprising.

Through a mixture of the enchantment of its physical setting and the unusual social structure, Cambridge seems to be a place to dream creative dreams, to think impossible things, to fantasize, to play with ideas. I have let fly a thousand intellectual arrows and though most have hit no target, no one has told me to stop the flow of what must at times have seemed to others somewhat crazy ideas. Cambridge is highly tolerant of mistakes, errors and wasted time.

This atmosphere encourages creativity. The career structure has been rather flat for many centuries. Although it has changed quite dramatically in the last twenty years with many more personal Readerships and Chairs, and the post of Senior Lecturer, the differences in salaries are not as great in most institutions. Once a person is a Fellow of a College, there is not much further to strive for in terms of promotion, except perhaps the headship of a College. So almost all of a person's energies do not go into career-related activities but rather into trying to teach well and understand difficult subjects.

*

The creativity in Cambridge also arises from the absence of strong barriers between skills and disciplines. The largest innovations and discoveries are made when hitherto discrete and distant areas of knowledge are brought together. This is normally difficult because of academic specialization. To penetrate deep into a problem requires years of training. Yet sheer technique and hard work cannot force a new solution. Findings from other disciplines with which one is only slightly conversant may be necessary to solve the largest problems.

What I have noticed from interviewing successful Cambridge scientists is the way they seem to move almost effortlessly between high-level skills in several disciplines. A cosmologist would know enough chemistry, biology, physics, and mathematics to answer specialized questions in his own field. A wide-ranging anthropologist whom I know is pretty fluent not only in the outlines of a number of cultures, but also history, linguistics, literature and archaeology.

This inter-disciplinary breadth is encouraged by the collegiate system. In many universities I have visited, you tend only to meet people in your own or very closely related disciplines. In Cambridge as an undergraduate your friends are from many disciplines and later at High Table you will normally be sitting with scientists, philosophers, classicists and others outside your own sphere. You soon learn how much you have in common, but also what divides you. You are required to explain clearly and simply the problems you are trying to solve to intelligent outsiders and this often clarifies your own thoughts. Life in the College can become a collective, long-term, interdisciplinary seminar. You have insights into the latest work in a broad range of subjects and an easy and equal access based on long-term acquaintance, friendship and shared responsibilities.

I cannot think of a more creative way to encourage the easy passage across barriers and the possibility of a sudden insight from a distinct and quite distant discipline. The very big problems, from the secret of life to the patterns of history or the universals of human cultures, can only be approached by using all the accumulated wisdom and insights of thousands of years of human thought. This bank of ideas is to be found in the physical libraries, laboratories and computers, but also in the virtual libraries, laboratories and computers of interesting minds.

*

The economist and philosopher Adam Smith believed that the major drives towards discovery arose from curiosity, or 'wonder and surprise'. A person is faced with a puzzle. How are two apparently unrelated phenomena so obviously linked at some deeper level? What makes things fall? What is the smallest element in the world? What makes humans so aggressive? The mind is intrigued and puzzled and tries to come up with a solution. The central spirit of a University is clearly curiosity, since most of academic life is the attempt to solve puzzles and problems. Having solved one major conundrum, the mind is faced immediately with the next.

The Cambridge educational system is based on two strands. One is Greek thought, which was unusual in encouraging people to question and to seek for new answers to old problems. The second was a medieval (English) legal tradition which encouraged confrontational argument in pursuit of a convincing answer to difficult questions. These wound round each other and gave rise to that pursuit of knowledge which is the essence of the Renaissance and the Scientific Revolution.

The man who mapped out this *New Atlantis*, and the way it might be attained, was another Cambridge educated figure, Francis Bacon. In his method for testing theories against facts, of observing natural phenomena in order to penetrate to the hidden but universal laws behind the surface of things, he charted a new world to be discovered and provided some of the tools for the exploration.

Bacon's methods are only part of the necessary set of technologies of thought and that inspiration, guessing and hypothesizing are just as important. Yet Bacon's whole endeavour, and that of thousands of other thinkers in the west from Leonardo da Vinci to Einstein, is founded on a basic curiosity about how the world works. It is the curiosity of the child who asks the simple questions and will not be put off by superficial answers.

The normal tendency in centres of thought is that curiosity, being a childish obsession, is irrelevant. Many forces in an academic setting suppress it. It may be an over-powerful ruling elite within the institution who crushes the next generation whose ideas threaten their power. This I have never experienced to any serious extent in Cambridge where the complex balance of Colleges and University protects the individual and gives him or her the independence to challenge orthodoxy.

Curiosity is suppressed by routinization, by teaching and researching the same subject year after year. There is something of this in Cambridge, but certainly in my own discipline there is always a demand for lectures on new topics, new courses, new doctoral students with new themes and areas. This makes for freshness, even when it leads into an opposite danger, that of over-stimulation and of too many possibilities.

Cynicism and a feeling that all is either known, or impossible to know, suppress curiosity. The wonderful experience of working in a University whose history is strewn with constant new and important discoveries, of new disciplines springing up, stories of how our world has been reshaped by chance breakthroughs, tends to diminish cynicism and world weariness.

I have found Cambridge to be a mostly fresh and hopeful place. People are aware of the impossibility of knowing anything for certain. As philosophers and scientists they have foreshadowed the doubts of post-modern scepticism for many centuries. Yet many of those I meet still retain that freshness which we find in the intellectual renaissance of the Middle Ages. They have the belief that the world is full of clues to yet unsolved mysteries and that we have the chance in our lifetime to contribute a little to their solution. They share the hopefulness of a child, or of a Newton likening himself to a boy standing by the sea of knowledge and casting in a few small pebbles.

Curiosity can also be dampened by frustration, the sense that one does not have enough time, data, rewards or interest to make the search worthwhile. Again I have found that Cambridge has been wonderful in these respects. I have set out on a dozen or more curiosity driven projects during my time in Cambridge. What are the origins and nature of English individualism? What is the culture of capitalism? Where did freedom come from? What is the nature of love? How does Japan work? Why has tea conquered the world? What are the effects of glass? These are a few of my intellectual puzzles.

In order to make some progress and to feel that curiosity will not lead into a dead end, I have needed time. Although highly pressured, the reasonable vacations and sabbatical system in Cambridge has meant that I have found the time. Time can be generated if one learns the tricks of concentrating, using small morsels of time, dividing up the work into different levels that can be done in different time frames.

Yet the time would be less fruitfully spent without the stimulus of other resources. The conversation and collaboration with others on the search, especially those who at first seem far distant from us, has been mentioned. A second is the structure of teaching. Many see research and teaching as oppositional, as did Cardinal Newman in his *The Idea of a University*. Indeed, if one is overloaded with undergraduate supervisions it can indeed drain creativity. On the whole, however, I have found that the pressure to learn new things, to explain things simply, to learn about what interests younger people, has been a stimulus. Indeed, I have noted that those who go off into pure research posts, or out of formal academic life, because they believe they will do more, often produce less. The grit that produces the pearls seems to be missing.

Another resource is data—sources, records and accumulated information. Cambridge is full of sources of inspiration. The obvious ones are the libraries. I have often been able to turn a hunch into a worked idea because I could easily find the books. I have also realized how serendipitous and chancy knowledge is by library research.

For example, when studying the impact of glass I found that there were a number of bounded but limited aspects of glass, each represented in separate libraries and museums. Scientific, artistic, recreational glass was exhibited and analysed in different places and even the University Library has a very limited range. Yet by being able to walk between half a dozen fine libraries and museums I could find all I needed.

Cambridge is a vast cabinet of curiosities, as museums used to be called, places which serve to generate and provide clues to the solution of curiosities. For a scientist, no doubt, the situation is similar. Neighbouring laboratories, what is happening on another floor or building, a chance conversation at High Table which starts a long and fruitful collaboration, all are part of a concentrated yet distributed mental and emotional machine which is 'good to think with'.

There are enough boundaries and protections—the thick doors, the exclusive clubs, the set apart times and places, the libraries and laboratories, the sabbaticals and research periods—to enable sustained bursts of creative work. Yet it is also not too bounded. The constant changes in its population with visitors and students and now the Internet revolution means that Cambridge is also 'leaky'. Cambridge is part of a vast international network and its prestige allows it to link to the best departments and universities. It is simultaneously a small provincial city and a place where big questions are being asked and curiosity extends out to all parts of the world.

*

I find that when I am involved in trying to write or to solve a difficult problem I become especially absent-minded and forgetful. This donnish forgetfulness is a well-known stereotype. It is said that the wife of the great scientist J.J. Thomson, discoverer of the electron, noticed one day that he had gone out leaving his normal clothes by his bedside. She had to search for the presumably pyjama-clad Master of Trinity through the early morning Cambridge streets.

When contemplating the deeper mysteries one may forget the smaller things. Adam Smith, who, like a few people I know in Cambridge used to go around mumbling to himself, was known to crumble up bread instead of tea and put it into the teapot, to the consternation of his guests. He also used to wander off in his nightclothes along the Fife coast as he tried to discover the causes of *The Wealth of Nations*.

Newton said, to solve the 'Riddle of the Universe' one has to think about it all the time and the concentration is not easy. Yet this ability to concentrate intensely on one subject seems to be a distinctive characteristic of many great Cambridge figures. Long and intense concentration, the 99 per cent of perspiration required for a break-through, is something at which the English excel. Writing to Mrs Grote, Tocqueville noted 'What you say of the simple character of the English is true. Their perception is just, somewhat narrow, but clear: they see only what they look at; they do well only one thing at a time'.[1]

A particularly outstanding example of single-minded dogged pursuit of incredibly complex solutions is the work of Fred Sanger, who not once but twice did the amazingly arduous and long task of sequencing (by hand) first insulin and then a phage. The concentration of James Frazer, the anthropologist who reportedly worked a dozen hours a day, 364 days a year (he took off Christmas Day), for over twenty years in order to write the twelve volume anthropological work, *The Golden Bough*, is another.

*

This prodigious concentration is related to two features of English character which particularly struck foreign observers. One is individualism. This has been a theme of my life's work since my book on *The Origins of English Individualism*. I was struck by the extraordinary fact that from before the founding of Cambridge and up to the present the English have behaved as if societies are made up of individuals rather than groups. Each person, like Robinson Crusoe on his island, is thought of as a fully formed, independent, microcosm of English society with an innate soul, innate rights and duties, and a stable and fixed personality.

As I looked from Nepal, Japan and China, at this set of billiard-ball people, bouncing against each other over time, I was amazed.

[1] Tocqueville, *Memoir*, II, 365.

Almost all civilizations and societies put the group first. They believe that relationships come before the individual. Yet in English law from the thirteenth century at least, as well as in English language, religion and other aspects of life, the separate English person has gone against this usual pattern.

Although it is a myth that we are independent of others—and all of the Cambridge thinkers I have encountered are obviously embedded in knowledge networks—the important thing is that they largely feel free, independent and able to pursue their intellectual interests without too much constraint from any larger group.

*

The second feature is positivism. Positivism means the belief that there are stable 'facts' and 'values' out in the 'real' world. The English legal requirement to take an oath to 'tell the truth, the whole truth and nothing but the truth' is based on the positivistic belief that a single, discoverable, 'truth' exists. Such a belief also lies at the root of the whole scientific tradition in England from well before the time when Francis Bacon's blueprint of how science should be pursued was elaborated. It was incorporated into the Royal Society and is clearly present as an article of faith in the minds of most of those, whether social scientists or scientists, whom I have talked to at length about their work.

As George Orwell observed, 'In England such concepts as justice, liberty and objective truth are still believed in. They may be illusions, but they are very powerful illusions.'[2] The English seem to believe that 'truth' and 'facts' exist independently of the observer. They have, of course, been aware of how people lie and that we all construct our worlds to a considerable extent—as Bishop Berkeley noted in relation to his tree. But deeper there is a faith, unprovable but absolutely necessary for science ('God does not play tricks' as Einstein put it) that there are real truths to be discovered. Without such a

[2]Orwell, *Lion and the Unicorn*, 45.

faith, who would devote huge energy and a whole life to 'science' in the widest sense?

If one is assailed by what a Cambridge philosophical anthropologist Ernest Gellner called the 'epistemological plague'— extreme constructivism and relativism—it makes all the tremendous effort pointless. If laboratories, for example, are just social organizations which are no different in their essence from a shop or a football club, why bother? If, in the end, each person's perception of the world is equally valid and equally futile, why go on? The courage to struggle on into uncharted seas requires faith, a hunch that a distant land really exists to be found and that finding it will somehow enrich the world.

Much of what an academic does seem pretty futile. It is for much of the time a long, petty, grinding, activity, achieving nothing or repeating the stale discoveries of the past. The rewards, if there are any, are often twenty years away. The book, experiments or article drags on; the hair grows grey; some of your friends smile behind your back at your apparently wasted life. It is easy to lose hope, to become cynical, to retreat into something which has some short-term outcome such as administration.

Yet the single-minded pursuit of reliable knowledge, which is found in the work of many great scientists, is something that Emerson noted about the English. 'For they have a supreme eye to facts, and theirs is a logic that brings salt to soup, hammer to nail, oar to boat, the logic of cooks, carpenters, and chemists, following the sequence of nature, and one on which words make no impression.'[3]

Only a blinding sense of renewed wonder, of amazement, of curiosity, as Einstein often remarked, can brush away these doubts. Only a sense that the world is *not* full of illusion, of *maya* as Hindu or Buddhist philosophies tell us, can justify the struggle to continue the quest, to return to the foundations of one's discipline and to create something new.

[3]Emerson, *English Traits*, 65.

Cambridge has somehow managed to remain young in its increasing old age, and to give a sense of reality amidst all its fantasy and magic. It continues to delight, amuse, irritate and stimulate those who come into contact with it and will hopefully do so for many generations to come.

DISCOVERY

On the evening of 28 February 1953 a small group of people were drinking together at the far end of the *Eagle* pub in Cambridge. Another member of the group arrived in considerable excitement and announced 'Gentlemen. We have discovered the secret of life!'

That the announcement of the discovery of the double helical structure of DNA should be made in a pub is perhaps odd. What is even more odd is that Francis Crick was right. Though few saw the implications straight away, the famous discovery did indeed penetrate to the heart of how life is created and replicated. We need to remember, however, that this was the culmination of numerous discoveries in many fields of science and mathematics over five hundred years.

The story of DNA is only one amongst a host of important discoveries associated with people who have passed through Cambridge or worked for long periods there. The roll call of great scientists includes William Gilbert, Francis Bacon, William Harvey, Isaac Newton, Charles Darwin, James Clerk Maxwell, J.J. Thomson, Ernest Rutherford and Paul Dirac. Cambridge scientists won over eighty Nobel prizes in the twentieth century.

Why has there been this concentration of intellectual energy in this small town, bursting forth from time to time in many different

Francis Crick and James Watson

Francis Crick and James Watson with their model of the double helix of DNA which they discovered in 1953. They represent the more than eighty Nobel Prize winning scientists who have been associated with Cambridge in the twentieth century, continuing the tradition which was above all inaugurated by Isaac Newton in the seventeenth century.

fields, a set of explorations which spreads well beyond purely academic subjects?

Hard as it is to give a sense of how education in the widest sense works in Cambridge, it is even harder to describe the conditions which have led to a sustained intellectual endeavour, the background and chance events which lead to major achievements. I have discovered something of what happens in

Ernest Rutherford's Room in the Old Cavendish Laboratory in the 1930s

This was the room where many of his most dramatic experiments and discoveries were made, including some of the final work before the first splitting of the atom. At that time, much of the equipment was still designed and put together by the experimental scientist.

the intersection of lives and works in the roughly eighty film interviews which I have done with Cambridge figures in most of the arts, humanities, social sciences and sciences. The words and expressions of those I have talked to convey something of the excitement as well as the strain, the play of place and traditions and the chance encounters which lie behind true discoveries.[1] When the words from these interviews are transcribed onto paper, however, they become like dried pebbles from the sea—the magic is lost. So let me approach the question of the conditions of

[1]The interviews are up on *www.alanmacfarlane.com* and many also on the 'Ayabaya' channel on YouTube.

intellectual creativity in a different way, from my own observations and experience.

*

Cambridge has always struck me as a place where the role of chance is especially evident. Of course luck is always present in our lives, but because this small University town is a simplified stage, the chance meetings and encounters which take a person in a completely new direction tend to be remembered and located in space and time. This comes across in many of the interviews with famous thinkers who recount that moment of excitement and chance encounter and I remember many of my own such moments.

The sense that one's progress through Cambridge is full of chances is exacerbated not only by the impressed memory of the exact place and moment. Much of one's life in Cambridge is a quest, a search, a looking for solutions to intellectual problems. In such a journey it is the unexpected and distant encounters that matter—like a medieval knight, in the midst of a wild wood, at midnight, when least expecting a clue.

In many occupations such chance encounters are less likely. People move around within an invisible bubble of the like-minded and the chance of meeting and collaborating at a deep level with someone well away from this bubble are slight. It is possible to do it by going a long way away, as I have done in strong working relationships and friendships with people in Nepal, Japan and China. But within England, the security, equality, trust and curiosity which are needed to forge these bonds across large areas of mutual difference are usually absent.

I have found that Cambridge is not only unusually rich in distinguished and interesting people, but that being part of a 'club' makes it easier to communicate with others within this social unit. In my own experience I have found it easy to work between history, anthropology, sociology, computing, film, museums and demography.

In terms of occupations, the gap between being an academic, businessman, and in the media is quite small.

If we think of ourselves as positively or negatively charged atoms, the greatest effect will be when we attract or become attracted to people or ideas at a distance. We can make useful breakthroughs and contributions to knowledge by working within a paradigm, within a discipline, yet what has been notable about Cambridge is that it has produced an unusually large number of thinkers who have elaborated new paradigms—in poetry, philosophy, biology, physics, economics, anthropology and many other fields. It has an unusual number of 'founding fathers' (and a few 'founding mothers' are emerging).

The wonderful thing I have found about Cambridge is that the chance of meeting really exciting and wondering minds either in the University or through its prestige and links is high. It is a rich sea, with numerous small, middling and large fish and much nutriment. The prestige, excellent facilities and general morale of the place can turn chance into something that looks like design.

Darwin's theory has been reformulated as 'random variation and selective retention'. Cambridge is full of random variation. The rapid movement of the ideas and energy of excellent students and many visitors and research projects is constantly shaking it up. Yet it also allows the stability and security to turn chance variation into selective retention. It was a chance that I met Ken Moody in 1973 and started to work on the overlap between computers, history and anthropology. Once it had happened, it was not too difficult to sustain a partnership with the help of three generations of computer students during a period of thirty years.

It has often been stated that 'fortune favours the prepared mind'. The preparation of the mind is one thing—but the chances of fortune blowing a rich seed into such a mind is particularly high in Cambridge. One obvious reason for this is its high quality. It is like playing with very good players in an exciting game—and this includes one's students.

All of us have had the experience of dull, conformist and dreary encounters, occasionally enriched by something unusual. Even in the most humdrum committee or meeting I sense in Cambridge that many of the people in the room are more intelligent than I am, have fascinating insights into worlds of which I know little, and could provide wonderful conversations and insights if, by chance, we found ourselves together on a long journey.

*

Einstein remarked that 'Unless an idea starts off as absurd, there is no hope for it'. I like this because it reminds us of the less well-known, but more exciting side of academic life. This is also caught in the title of Crick's autobiography *What Mad Pursuit*.

Like many others, I grew up with the image that most of the major achievements in the arts and sciences were based on the patient and logical accumulation of 'facts' or 'data'. In my own early research I believed that the researcher was like an archaeologist. He or she goes out and gathers fragments of information, whether bits of the past from documents, lost fragments of texts as a literary critic, pieces of behaviour and attitude as an anthropologist or, I imagined, observational data as a scientist. René Descartes in his *Essay on Method* described how one moved from the known to the unknown, moved logically forward, broke a problem into its constituent parts and then assembled the jigsaw at the end.

Of course all these things are necessary. I still believe that 'facts' exist. We do need to explore, gather, synthesize, arrange and test. The model here is the immense labour of logic and testing of an F.W. Maitland, Sir James Frazer, Fred Sanger or Joseph Needham, synthesizing a huge quantity of 'facts'.

Yet, in the end, to find something new and important, to open an as yet unopened or even unperceived trap door, to change a paradigm, to see something that has never been seen before, needs something additional. Various names have been given to this— intuition, guesswork, an absurd hunch, a way-out analogy. This is

F.W. Maitland

F.W. Maitland, Downing Professor of the Laws of England from 1888 to 1906, represents the many thinkers in the fields of the humanities and social sciences who have been associated with Cambridge. A historian, legal theorist and political philosopher, Maitland outlined better than any other the way in which Cambridge is based on trust and Trusts. [painting by Beatrice Lock in 1906]

what differentiates the patient march of 'normal' science from those paradigmatic shifts which alter our world.

What I love above all about the history of Cambridge is that there are dozens of cases of people who have moved beyond the safety of the known and the sensible, to the dangerous, absurd, crazy, unlikely waters of the unknown. There are Columbuses and Captain Cooks of the mind and I move not only among their ghosts but have also met a number of them in the flesh.

There are many reasons why few people attempt to pursue the absurd. They lack the self-confidence; they do not have the time or encouragement to turn unlikely hunches into proofs (as Newton had to do when he turned his intuitive solutions into recognizable mathematics); they lack a set of equally crazy colleagues who argue and discuss and shoot down the absurd arguments that do not work. To execute the unexpected move, cut through and across the barriers and outside the blinkers, abandon long-held truths which are hidden obstacles to major changes of direction is dangerous and difficult.

It is much safer, and often more comfortable, and more pleasant for one's family and friends, to steer the well-charted, moderately rewarding course, to earn the praise of one's equals rather than the reputation of someone with a wild gleam in their eyes, a crazy preacher speaking in tongues. Yet Cambridge tolerates the wild prophet, the playful eccentric, the thinker of a thousand impossible things before breakfast.

*

I have found this to be true in my own experience of the University. I could let my interests and hunches free. I was not dissuaded from what, at first sight, seemed to be crazy ideas, by the pressures to produce, to conform, to be part of a tight closed group. It was assumed that curiosity should be allowed a free rein. I had seen this in operation with my first mentor and head of Department in Cambridge, Jack Goody, a model of lateral, somewhat eccentric, thought, who turned his attention to many fields and wrote interestingly about a multitude of subjects including, love, kinship, property, flowers, cooking, technology and Islam.

What Jack Goody had discovered, and I found from these thought experiments, is that the mind's best work is done by prospecting widely, by following the suggestion that 'it is better to be roughly right rather than precisely wrong'. The mind works like a slash and burn farmer, by moving on after a few years to a new, if somewhat related, topic. The excitement of real research, and the insights at a deeper level, comes in the attempt to understand something just on the edge of one's competence. To go over a subject again and again, just as growing the same crops on the same land year after year, leads to staleness and loss of productivity.

Of course, the absurdities have to be tempered. One fires off thousands of ideas and solutions and most of them come to nothing. Yet a few survive the honest and highly critical comments of one's friends and advisors. And because they started as unlikely, they are intriguing and may uncover hitherto unsuspected connections: in my case trust and modernity, tea and the industrial revolution, glass and the Renaissance.

It is indeed a 'mad pursuit', but without a little madness, and a little method in the madness, the deeper understanding of our world will not occur. There seems little justification in keeping a body of thinkers in existence if their only task is to rethink the thoughts of their ancestors. So we encourage our students to try out new ideas in their essays, in discussions, in their art, drama and sports. And they hopefully end up in a world where they can continue their unconventional explorations and stumble on that great pleasure of seeing other worlds where no one has ever been before, 'silent upon a peak in Darien'.

What this amounts to is the fact that intellectual activities involve risk; risk that one may be wrong, make a fool of oneself, waste years on a false clue and waste other people's time and money. There are also practical dangers—laboratory accidents, litigation over copyright or misadventures 'in the field'.

What I have appreciated over the years is that the University has walked the thin line between under and over caution pretty well. Intellectual risks are not discouraged and it is up to the individual to take their own risks and to bear the consequences, though the University provides some guidance and longer-term support. Yet both in relation to intellectual and practical risks, the rise of a risk-averse, health and safety dominated, culture has been kept within bounds.

*

There is a saying that 'A scientist is a device for turning coffee into theorems'. And indeed there is a high emphasis in Cambridge on liquid stimulants—coffee, tea, beer, sherry, wine and port. The role these play in the sociability and creativity of an institution like Cambridge are worth considering.

In many cultures, one or more of these invigorating or mildly intoxicating substances are banned, as with alcohol in Islam and in some Christian sects. In Cambridge there may be teetotal dons, but there is no general ban. Indeed those who abstain from one or more of these are the exception and often have to explain their position.

Coffee is a powerful stimulant which can help a tired student or researcher squeeze in some extra effort. Ideas do not keep office hours. It is often late at night that the essay has to be written, the lecture prepared, the computer is free. Then coffee spurs us on. Coffee is obviously a sociable drink and Cambridge has a large number of coffee shops where tourists congregate or one might entertain a visitor in sociable warmth and shared appreciation of this stimulating and relaxing drink. I have never forgotten the liberation of moving from a boarding school to Oxford and entertaining people to coffee and biscuits. The coffee and mints round off a special dinner in College and bring the mind back to earth after a long evening of wine and talk.

Tea is different. It is more associated with 'Englishness', more ritualized in its preparation, serving and drinking. The tea party with colleagues or students is often a more formal experience. It is often associated with food, sandwiches, the 'honey' of Rupert Brooke's poem, the bread or scones toasted by the gas fire in the long Cambridge winters. It is a consoling, relaxing, invigorating and restoring drink.

After an exhausting outing on the river or rugby field, after a tiring lecture or day of teaching, the 'good old British cup of tea' is as appreciated in Cambridge as anywhere. When the water supplies of Cambridge were polluted, the boiled water and phenolics in the tea helped many generations of Cambridge dons and students avoid the dysentery, typhoid and other diseases which drinking cold water would have brought. Without tea, Cambridge, like all of England, could not have thrived in the way it did. Tea gives a sense of peace and self-confidence. It has also been shown to improve the memory and associational powers of the brain by up to 20 per cent, so it may have had dramatic effects on numerous intellectual efforts.

*

Like much of England, the Cambridgeshire countryside a hundred years ago was full of a wide range of places where one could drink beer. These varied from tiny alehouses serving a few neighbouring houses, of which there were many in my fen parish, up to the grand coaching inns which can still be seen along main roads or in the big pubs such as the *Eagle*, the *Bath*, the *Blue Boar* (now gone) and other inns in Cambridge. Also each College was a grand inn, with a wide range of beers and ales, with its own alcohol licence issued by the magistrates and nowadays with the College bars where so much intellectual and social exchange takes place.

The mind is like a rubber band. It is stretched to capacity by intense intellectual work, by reading, writing, teaching, and experimenting. Yet it also needs to relax from time to time. The pubs and student bars are one of the main places, alongside games and the arts, where this can occur. After a long day in the computer laboratories or Old Cavendish laboratories, the academics repair to the *Eagle* or the *Bath*. After an intense seminar the anthropologists adjourn to King's College Bar, as they have done for the thirty-five years I have been associated with the Department.

The huddled charm of a busy bar, the welcome glow of a good ale, all induce the nearest many Cambridge people find to what Durkheim describes as the spring of religion—effervescence. The difficulties, blocks, puzzles seem to resolve themselves. The imagination is released to play more intuitively with hypotheses. It is possible to go more directly to one's inner thoughts and hunches. Friendship, real exchange of ideas and emotions is present; as it is for another buttoned-up tribe, the Japanese, when they retreat to their sushi bars and drink saké. Many a new seed of a way through a problem has been hatched with a half-full jug of beer by one's side through 800 years of very English drinking at Cambridge.

Fortunately beer is traditionally quite mild. Some of my more practised friends can drink three or four pints a night and not lose their ability to walk in a straight line. It is usually drunk slowly and meditatively, creaming off the wealth of the English countryside to obtain good nutrition and the medicinal value of hops. That England was able to devote roughly half of its grain products to the making of drink, something no other country until recently could have dreamt of doing, is the key to a very special pleasure.

*

Then there is wine. Medieval England was not merely an ale country, but deeply involved in the wine world of France. English wool was traded down the Cam and Ouse to France and in return wines from that country, particularly Bordeaux, flowed back. The cellars of the Colleges are famous and often valuable. When, twenty years ago, I was involved in a project to film life in a Cambridge College we were allowed to film in the chapel, library, kitchens, everywhere except the wine cellars, which were deemed too vulnerable (and sacred?) to allow this.

Christmas is celebrated by tempting offers of special wines, feasts accompanied by a dizzying array. I distinctly remember nearly forty years ago after my first attendance at an important King's Committee, the delicious white wine which was served afterwards and the sudden shock of realizing that I was tasting something I had not experienced before.

There is an old saying, *in vino veritas*, 'in wine—truth', and I have always been intrigued by the different interpretations one can put on this. A good meal and good wine with Fellows in a College indeed does give one a sense that one can speak the truth, be honest, close the gap between the constantly watchful self-control of ordinary life, and one's real feelings. One can tell the truth more directly, and learn truths that would normally be kept hidden.

This is not surprising. The synapses of the brain which facilitate our thoughts are chemically altered by stimulants contained in all the drinks I have discussed. People have recorded this for many substances from mescaline and LSD to the opium which stimulated Coleridge and De Quincey. The Cambridge-trained poet A.E. Houseman records that he would have a large lunch, with lots of beer and then, slightly foggy, go for a walk. Often in this state whole stanzas of his poem the *Shropshire Lad* would fall fully formed into his mind. Wine and beer intoxicates and relaxes, it is an alternative way in which to put the mind into another gear, an alternative to walking, having a shower, gardening, sport and all those other devices for altering our viewpoint on the world.

Furthermore, these social drinks are expressive. Much of Cambridge life is about distance and closeness, keeping the freedom of separateness, yet communicating closely with people who become friends. Wine expresses this, just as the wine of communion expresses closeness and the integration with Christ. The circling of the port after High Table, the offering of sherry to visitors and undergraduates, the glass of wine at the end of a seminar or book launch, express and also create closeness. As in all things English, it also expresses class. The code of sherry, for example, mirrors class—the drier the more upper class.

*

One of the main architects of the idea of the clockwork universe, Isaac Newton, also gave us some of our deepest understanding of light. In order to do his experiments he meticulously ground his own lenses. In my interviews of leading scientists I have been impressed by their continuation of this 'hands-on' involvement, not only using complex tools for discovery, but also making and adapting such tools.

There is a normal tendency for priests, nobles and intellectuals to withdraw into an abstract realm, as far away from the material world as possible. A Brahmin cannot do any physical labour, many Buddhists eschew practical work, and the nobility of much of continental Europe were early examples of that 'leisure class' which Thorstein Veblen brilliantly satirized. The purer the mathematics, philosophy or poetry, the further removed it is from any possible application, the higher the status.

Yet observers noted that the English, including their academics and their gentry class from whom they came, seemed curiously drawn to doing things with their hands. They experimented on their farms with the crops that made their agricultural revolution. They tinkered in the sheds and laboratories with the gadgets which gave them their industrial revolution. 'The bias of the nation is a passion for utility. They love the lever, the screw, and pulley, the Flanders draught-horse, the waterfall, wind-mills, tide-mills; the sea and the wind to bear their freight-ships.' 'For, the Englishman has accurate perceptions;' Emerson elaborates 'loves the axe, the spade, the oar, the gun, the steam-pipe; he has built the engine he uses.'[2]

This happened all over Britain, for instance among the members of the Lunar Society in the eighteenth century that included James Watt, Matthew Boulton and others. Despite its intellectualism and snobbery, Cambridge was part of this broader interest in combining intellectual with practical activities, dabbling with the 'shifting of atoms' in engineering, chemistry, applied mathematics and design. Charles Babbage, Darwin and many others were not just abstract thinkers; they also built and collected and 'got their hands dirty' in a way which would have shocked and even disgusted many of their elite equivalents in other civilizations.

I have always found this tradition of combining the abstract and theoretical with the practical, hands-on, gadget-using and constructing aspects of work a particularly rewarding experience in Cambridge. Although once or twice my colleagues have commented in an amused or bemused way on an office filled with wires, computers, scanners, cameras, their attitude is tolerant. In practical terms the College and University have always supported what can be a costly involvement with gadgets to record and analyse a changing world.

I recently interviewed the astronomer Martin Rees and was struck by his forceful assertion that most of the developments in his field were the result of improvements in technology, the increasing power of telescopes and computers. This is equally true in slightly different ways in much of the path-breaking work in chemistry, physics, molecular biology, medicine and even pure mathematics. Less well known is the way it has also deeply affected the arts and

[2]Emerson, *English Traits*, 67, 177.

social sciences, as I have experienced in anthropology and history.

In order to remain at the forefront of what is happening, it is not enough to wait for others to devise and develop the technologies for research and communication. If I had done so, much of my work on the reconstruction of historical village records and the recording and analysis of other civilizations would never have been done. Not only would the technology have come too late, but also without really understanding it from the inside I would not have seen its potential before it became widely available. I had to learn how to set up information retrieval systems, film and edit, set up websites, become acquainted with 'YouTube' and 'Facebook', make electronic books and many other skills which are half theoretical and half practical.

The Christian monastic tradition, have always valued a combination of the practical and the spiritual. The respect for hard manual labour, the interest in labour-saving and knowledge-producing devices, which one finds from St Benedict onwards, was built into Cambridge from the start. However, as we have seen, though this seems to be a necessary origin, in many parts of Europe it died out, but has been preserved in Cambridge.

*

Cambridge is a Museum, but not just a passive one with static objects in glass cases. Rather it is like the computers which were to a considerable extent dreamt of and devised in Cambridge. It thinks, adapts, and changes with the world. Yet the programs which run it are often, in essence, centuries old. They were laid down early on, but were general and flexible enough to absorb the vast transformation that would happen during its eight hundred year history.

Like the ship of the Argonauts on its long voyage, while Cambridge has constantly had to be patched, bits replaced because rotten, new bits added for further journeys, the structure, the design, the fact that it is a ship of a certain kind, has remained remarkably unchanged. It is recognizably the same, in the way that a venerable old oak tree of eight hundred years continuous growth is still in many ways the little oak sapling of its youth. And what it stands for, its largely unstated goals which can never be captured in a 'mission statement', and the customs which can never be adequately described, is a set of practices and assumptions which have not fundamentally altered.

Cambridge stands for curiosity, openness, fellowship, wonder, humour, playfulness, awe, delight, argument, competitiveness, modesty, subversion, ceremonial, kindness, tolerance, beauty, utility, liberty, conformity and a whole bundle of often colliding and clashing values. Those who have navigated its still pools and rapids are attracted to many of these features in differing times and to different degrees.

Combined with its charm and a feeling of otherworldly magic, it seldom fails to make a deep impression, even if a person appears to forget or reject it. Like any powerful parent, it affects the rest of their lives, whether they like it or not. It evokes strong emotions.

Above all, Cambridge gives me, and many, a sense of hope. Here is a place which has preserved a set of ideals within beautiful surroundings for over three quarters of a millennium. Much of the treasure it has accumulated is not in its physical buildings, but in what the Japanese would describe as 'living national treasures'. The poets, scientists, philosophers and others, dead or alive, are its greatest gift, along with the large number of students who have passed through it and gone on to their diverse careers.[3]

Alongside them are the cultural treasures, a set of manners, assumptions, and attitudes to life, which are not visible to the casual visitor. A guided tour of the museums and some of the Colleges, noting a few plaques to great thinkers, or a walk along the Backs will give a visitor a sense that much must lie beneath this surface. What lies deeper is the hidden culture and history of a small fenland city and university which has been one of the bridges into our twenty-first century world.

[3]There are partial lists of some of these people in various books and websites. I have compiled my own 'virtual tour' of Cambridge people and Colleges, which can be found by searching for 'Cambridge' on *www.alanmacfarlane.com*.